Don't Think of a Monkey

——————— *and*———————

Other Stories My Guru Told Me

Don't Think of a Monkey

———— *and* ————

Other Stories My Guru Told Me

Retold By

Swami Prakashananda

 *Sarasvati Productions*

Sarasvati Productions
43463 Columbia Ave.
Fremont, CA 94538

Don't Think of a Monkey
and
Other Stories My Guru Told Me

ISBN 1-886140-10-3
Library of Congress Catalog Card Number: 94-92302

Cover Design by Margaret DiMaria

Table of Contents

Preface

My Guru, Baba Muktananda, loved stories, and he had truly perfected the art of story telling. Having lived with him for many years I heard him narrate these stories many times. They served as a teaching vehicle, sometimes in a humorous way, for conveying certain spiritual truths, as well as the follies and antics of humanity.

Many of these stories have been narrated for thousands of years in India, as well as other parts of the Middle East, often modified by the narrator according to the needs of the moment. Some of the stories in this book are from the early *Upanishads*, and the great Indian epic, the *Mahabharata*. Stories and parables have always occupied an important place in the teachings of great masters. The fundamentals of the spiritual life are often conveyed in a humorous medium. Very often great truths are easily comprehended when narrated in such simple stories. I never tired of hearing my own Guru narrate these stories.

Some of Baba's favorite stories were those relating to the comical character of Mullah Nasrudin. As Nasrudin is known to be a great traveler, we find that he is variously known as the 'Hodja', the 'Mullah', or simply 'Nasrudin' throughout the Middle East, from the Mediterranean to India. He is referred to as either very stupid, or very wise, clever, and improbable in his exploits. I have therefore added a number of his tales scattered throughout this book.

I have chosen 108 of my favorite stories and hope that they will bring to you as much joy, and insight, as they have brought to me. Please note that none English terms have been generally italicized the first time they are used. Quite often the meaning of the word accompanies the narrative but a glossary of such terms can be found at the end of the book.

The Value Of A Saint

Once, the celestial sage Narada started on a pilgrimage to the heavenly abode of Lord Vishnu. One night he stopped at a small village and was given hospitality in the hut of a childless couple. The next morning, before he started out, the poor man said to him, "You are going to worship Lord Vishnu, so please ask him to bless us with a child." Narada agreed to do so.

When he reached the holy place, and after performing his obeisance, he said to the Lord, "That couple were very kind to me. Be merciful and give them a child." The Lord replied, with an air of finality, "It is not their destiny to have children." Accepting the Lord's reply Narada performed his worship and went home.

Some years later he set out on the same pilgrimage and happened to stop at the same village, and was once again given hospitality by the same couple. This time there were two small children playing in the courtyard of the hut.

"Whose children are these?" asked Narada. "They are mine," said the man proudly.

Narada was puzzled and questioned him further. The man went on to explain saying, "Soon after you left us, five years ago, a great *Siddha* came to our village and we put him up for the night. The next morning, before the saint left, he blessed my wife and me, and these are the fruits of his blessing."

When Narada heard this, he could not wait to reach the abode of Lord Vishnu. When he arrived there Narada shouted right from the entrance of the temple, "Did you not tell me that it was not in the destiny of that couple to have children? They now have two!"

When the Lord heard this, he laughed aloud and said, "Aah, that must be the work of a saint, Saints have the power to change destiny!"

Indeed, one can never underestimate the value of a saint. Due to their spiritual accomplishments they have the power to uplift those who take refuge in them.

Nachiketa
and
The Dialogue With Death

Vajasravas was an ambitious householder and he thought of performing a particular sacrifice which would bring him name and fame. Of the many different sacrifices that were current in those days, the one called *Viswajit*, meaning 'that which conquers the world', was one of them. It required that the sacrificer was to give away all his property as an offering.

Vajasravas decided to perform this sacrifice and started to give his possessions away to different *brahmins*, even though he actually had few possessions. His cattle were of an inferior quality, they were lean, and some were barren and others deformed.

His young son Nachiketa, observing his father, wondered about the validity of such an offering. Having great faith in himself, he thought of offering himself up in the sacrifice and approached his father asking, "Dear father, to whom will you offer me in this great sacrifice you are performing?"

His father, being preoccupied with the details of the ceremony, did not respond to his son's question.

Nachiketa again repeated the question, "Dear father, to whom will you offer me in this great sacrifice you are performing?"

Again the father did not respond, but one could see that he was getting annoyed.

Nachiketa asked the question a third time. This time his father, in anger, answered, "I offer you to *Yama*, the Lord of Death."

Nachiketa, being a young child, wondered at this strange reply from his father. He thought that he was not inferior to his brothers, but wondered of what use he would be to the god of Death.

But, being true to his word, and desirous of obeying his father's command, Nachiketa started for the abode of Death.

When he reached the underworld, he found that Yama was away from his home. Nachiketa decided to wait and he sat down at Yama's door. He waited there for three days without food and water. When Yama returned, he noticed the young boy waiting at his door steps. Hearing from his servants that the young Brahmin had been fasting for three days on his door steps, he knew that this did not bode well for the owner of the house, and immediately ordered food and water to be brought. Yama then offered Nachiketa a seat and requested him to ask for three wishes, one for each day of his fast.

"Oh Death," answered Nachiketa, "of the three wishes, the first that I ask is that my father should become peaceful and freed from anger towards me, and that he may recognize me when you return me to him."

Death replied, "This wish of yours will happen. Your father will be pleased to see you returning from the jaws of death, and will love you as before. He will also loose his anger and will sleep peacefully. Now ask your second boon."

Nachiketa said, "I have heard that in heaven there is no fear at all. You, Oh Death, are not there, and one does not experience old age. Freed from the pangs of hunger and thirst, and free from sorrow, all rejoice and are happy there. You, Oh King, know that fire sacrifice which leads to heaven. Being full of faith, I desire that you teach it to me, this is my second wish."

Yama was happy with Nachiketa's wish and he taught him the full knowledge of that ceremony, teaching him how to perform the sacrifice precisely. After hearing the teachings from Yama, Nachiketa repeated everything he had heard to make sure he had understood everything correctly.

Yama was so pleased that he said, "Oh Nachiketa, I will give you an extra boon. From now on, this fire ceremony will be called the Nachiketa sacrifice. Now ask for your third wish."

Nachiketa reflected for a moment and then said, "When a man dies, some say that he lives after death, while others say he does not. This subject is in dispute but is widely discussed. I would therefore like to know definitely from you the truth about it. This is the third of my wishes."

Yama answered, "This is a subtle subject and very difficult to understand. Even the gods were puzzled about it. So please don't press me for an answer. Choose another boon Oh Nachiketa."

But Nachiketa was not deterred. He said, "Oh Death, if what you say is true, that even the gods were once puzzled by this mystery, and that it is not easy to understand, surely there is no better teacher then you to explain it to me. I have no other wish then this."

Yama, testing the young Nachiketa again said, "Why don't you ask for sons and grandsons who will live for a hundred years. Ask for cattle, elephants, horses and gold. Choose a mighty kingdom and ask to rule the whole world. Or else ask for beautiful women, I'll give you celestial women that can not be found on the earth and you can enjoy pleasures beyond all thought. Or, choose any other boon you think equal to these, but please don't ask for the secret of death Oh Nachiketa!"

Nachiketa stood fast and said, "You, who are the destroyer of all things, yet offer me that which is ephemeral and lasts for but a day and wears out the senses. Keep your horses and cattle, your power and pleasures, what need have I for long life? Having seen your face, Oh Death, how shall I desire wealth. No, I only wish for the boon which I have chosen. Tell me therefore about that mystery of mysteries."

Lord Yama, having tested the resolve of Nachiketa was very

pleased. Seeing that his young disciple had faith, sincerity, was free from temptations, and, above all, had an intense desire to know the truth, he decided to impart to him the highest truth.

Yama said, "Dear child, two paths are always open to man, the path of good actions, and actions which are pleasant. They both have their own ends. Those who choose the path of goodness are blessed, while he who follows the pleasant path misses the goal. The wise, having examined both prefer the good, while the foolish, driven by desires prefer the pleasant to the good. You have spurned the path of sensual pleasures and have chosen the path of the spirit which brings permanent good to you. Ignorant fools who don't know that there is the other world of immortal bliss, are caught again and again in my net. The wise, however, are few and they follow the other path. It is no doubt a subtle and difficult path, the knowledge of it is very rare. Rare also are those who inquire about it, and it is only those who have realized it that can impart it to others. This truth can not be known by intellect and logic alone Oh Nachiketa.

"The wise man attains this ancient knowledge of the immanence of the spirit that pervades all things by the practice of meditation on the inner Self, called the *Atman*. He then goes beyond joy and sorrow. This Self lies beyond the duality's of pleasure and pain, success and failure, hot and cold. The Self lies hidden in the lotus of the heart Oh Nachiketa. The *Vedas* point to this goal and the various penance's and other spiritual practices aim at it alone. The mystic symbol of that Spirit is *Om*.

"That Supreme Spirit is neither ever born nor does it ever die. He is neither cause nor effect. This Ancient One is eternal, imperishable; though the body is destroyed, he is not killed.

"Smaller than the smallest, greater than the greatest, this Self forever dwells within the hearts of all. When a man is free from desire, his mind and senses purified, he beholds the glory of the Self and is without sorrow.

"This Self can not be known through the study of the scriptures, nor through subtlety of the intellect, nor even through vast learning. It is by the grace of the Spirit alone that one can be blessed with its knowledge, though all of these do help the process.

"If one has not abstained from bad deeds or controlled his senses and calmed his mind with the practice of meditation one cannot hope to know this Self.

"The human body is like a chariot and the soul is the charioteer. The senses are the horses and the sense-objects are the road along which they travel. The wise call the Self the enjoyer when he is united with the body, the senses, and the mind. A man who lacks discrimination and his mind is uncontrolled, his senses are unmanageable like uncontrolled horses. But he who can discriminate between the real and the false, whose mind is steady and whose heart is pure, reaches the goal, and having reached it is born no more.

"Few are they who look within themselves and try to find and realize the Self. Since at the time of creation, the Spirit went forth outward, therefore the mind and senses have the tendency to be engaged with the external world.

"The senses of the wise man obeys his mind, his mind obeys his intellect, his intellect obeys his ego, and his ego obeys the Self.

"Arise, awake, and approach the feet of the Master and know 'That'. In one's own heart that Self is clearly realized, as if seen in a mirror. When all the senses are stilled, when the mind is at rest, when the intellect does not waiver, that, say the wise, is the highest state.

"It is a difficult and narrow path to tread. The sages say it is sharp like the edge of a razor. But success is sure to those who strive to accomplish it Oh Nachiketa."

Nachiketa, having learned from the god of Death the path of yoga, achieved the knowledge of the Self, and was united with that Supreme Spirit. This dialogue with the Lord of Death was first narrated in the Katha Upanishad.

The Donkey Shrine

Nasrudin's father was the custodian of a well known *dargah*, which is the burial shrine of a great being. Many *Sufis* would stop there and Nasrudin would have wonderful conversations with them. Finally one day he also got the desire to wander about in search of Truth. His father had wanted him to remain at home and take over the charge of the shrine, but Nasrudin had made up his mind. His father finally relented and blessed Nasrudin and gave him a donkey for his travels. Nasrudin started out and he traveled to many places, he had visited many holy shrines and spent a great deal of time alone in the woods.

After many years of wandering, one day the donkey collapsed and died. Now, Nasrudin had become very attached to that donkey. After all, it had been his only companion for so many years. So it was not surprising that he became very sad and fell down on the ground crying, "Alas, my friend is dead, he has left me!"

Nasrudin was in such a pitiful condition that some people who had been passing by tried to comfort him and also started to cover the donkey with stones and mud. After sometime a sort of shrine had developed and Nasrudin just sat there still not knowing what to do and brooding over what had happened. People passing that way would stop and look at Nasrudin and wondered what was the matter. Some of them said that it must be a disciple meditating at his Guru's shrine, and they started to lay garlands of flowers at the shrine, and also left money. Soon many people started visiting the shrine and many priests also came. Business people soon arrived and opened flower and incense shops, fruit stands, and restaurants. More and more people came to worship there and finally a proper *Mosque* was built.

Eventually, news of this famous Mosque reached Nasrudin's village and his father. His father decided to visit this popular mosque and meet with the great *dervish* who was living there. When he arrived he looked around and was impressed with how large the shrine was. He tied up his donkey and asked to see the dervish. When he saw that it was his son, he went over and embraced him, feeling very happy. He said, "I'm so happy to know that you have become so famous and your fame even now continues to increase, but tell me, who is the great sufi buried under the shrine?"

Nasrudin said, "Well father, what can I say..." and he continued to narrate to his father the whole story about how the donkey he had giving him died, and how people buried it, and finally erected the mosque. His father, with a look of surprise exclaimed, "Allah is great, how mysterious are his ways, for the exact same thing happened to me."

Baba often narrated this story in order to illustrate two different points. The first was that one's pure feelings, and the fact that God is all pervasive, is all that is required for devotion to bear fruit, and not the place of worship. At other times, he would narrate this story in order to convey the importance of discrimination on the part of the seeker when searching for a true master.

The Guru's Lesson

Once a disciple asked his Guru, "Oh Master, please tell me how I can see God?" "Come with me," answered the Guru, "and I'll show you."

The Guru took the disciple to a nearby river, and both of them got into the water. All of a sudden, the master pressed the disciple's head under the water. After a few moments he released him and the disciple raised his head, gasping for air.

The Guru asked, "Well, how did it feel?"

The disciple said, "Oh! I thought I would die; I was frantically gasping for a breath of air."

The Guru said, "When you feel that way for God, then you'll know that you haven't long to wait for his vision."

In order to know God, and to have a glimpse of him, we must yearn for him with great intensity. It must be as if our life depended on it.

Prahlada
The Child Devotee

O nce there lived a demon by the name of Hiranyakashipu. He was so powerful that he over ran even the throne of *Indra,* the king of the gods. After performing intense austerities he received a boon from Brahma for power and dominion. He had also asked the creator not to be killed by the gods or demons, man or beast, neither during the day or at night, not on the earth or in the air, nor inside or outside a building.

The evil king Hiranyakashipu had brought the three worlds under his control. Displacing Indra and the other gods, he himself performed the functions of the sun, moon, air, waters and fire. He became the god of riches and the judge of the dead, having displaced *Kubera* and *Yama.* He took for himself all the sacrifices which were made to the gods, while the true deities wandered on the earth disguised as mere mortals.

Hiranyakashipu was inflated with pride, and he enjoyed whatever his senses desired. Having achieved this great task he declared that nowhere in the universe was there any god but himself.

Now this demon had a young son named Prahlada. Even though Prahlada was only a child and the son of an atheist, he himself was a great devotee of God. He was also kind and gentle to everyone. Even as a child, he set aside his toys and focused his mind on the meditation of *Hari,* the Lord. Being so overwhelmed with devotion he was not conscious of normal actions such as walking, sitting, eating, sleeping, drinking or speaking. Sometimes his consciousness would become agitated due to a feeling of longing for the Lord and he would begin to cry. Sometimes he would laugh in excitement in his meditation on Him; and sometimes he would sing aloud.

Now Prahlad's father, thinking that his son was being polluted by someone, decided to send him to school. He instructed the teacher to keep an eye on Prahlada and make sure that no one gave him any spiritual instructions. He wanted to keep his son away from religion. He desired that Prahlada should remain a worldly person like himself.

But Prahlada knew about God from an inner inspiration, and he would gather the other children of the demons around him and teach them to chant God's holy name. He would also tell them to give up their demonic nature and to show kindness and friendliness to all beings.

Hearing of these actions of his son, his father became furious. At first he took Prahlada on his lap and tried to dissuade him from remembering God, telling him that God did not exist.

Prahlada replied, "It is due to a polluted heart that one does not know God. Looking for guidance from those who regard the external objects as the aim of life, lost in worldly enjoyments, they cannot reach the feet of the Lord. Oh father, the Lord dwells in the whole universe, try to see him."

As Prahlada was speaking, his father was overwhelmed with rage. He ordered that his son should immediately be put to death. At first they tried to frighten him thinking that he would give up his beliefs but Prahlada remained calm and fearless. Even though his father tried to kill him in numerous ways, like drowning, setting him on fire, piercing him with different weapons and even poison, still he was not able to harm the child, as he was protected by the Lord of the universe.

Picking up a large sword, Hiranyakashipu said, "Oh ill mannered and stupid boy, relying on whose power did you violate my command? I, at whose wrath all the three worlds tremble with fear!"

Prahlada answered, "He on whom I rely is verily the source of all power, not only of me, but of yours as well. He is that force which keeps under control all creation, high and low, mobile an immobile. He is the Supreme Lord, the Eternal Spirit, the very essence of courage and intelligence. Oh Father, give up your demonic nature. There is no external enemy except one's own uncontrolled mind. People like you regard yourselves as conquerors of the three worlds, yet you have not even conquered the five senses and the mind."

Hiranyakashipu said, "Oh wretched child! Where is this Lord of the universe, if there be any other than I?"

Prahlada answered, "He is everywhere. I see him in all directions, in all objects, even in you Oh father."

"Is he even in this pillar?" scoffed Hiranyakashipu, pointing to one of the pillars in the assembly hall.

"Yes, He is seen there also," answered Prahlada, and he bowed to the pillar.

Hearing these words of Prahlada, his father said, "Then let him appear to me in any form he chooses," and struck the pillar with his sword. Suddenly a terrible roar was heard coming from the pillar, which immediately cracked, revealing an unusual creature. He was called *Narsimha*, the man-lion. His eyes were fierce like molten gold, and his face majestic with the dazzling hair of his mane. He had a tongue sharp like the blade of a razor, and it was flickering like a flame; his face struck terror with its frowning eye-brows. His mouth and nostrils were open and he appeared terrible with his parted jaws. He was huge in stature and had a short thick neck, broad chest and a slender waist. He was covered with hair, white like the rays of the Moon. He had numerous arms on either side, armed with claws. Grabbing a hold

13

of Hiranyakashipu, at the threshold of the assembly-hall, the creature picked him up and laid him on his thigh and tore open his chest and stomach with his claws, killing the demon instantly.

The creature had met all the conditions which had been imposed in order to kill the demon. For he was neither a god nor a demon, nor a human or beast. The time was dusk, and therefore neither day or night, and the creature placed the demon on his lap and so he was neither on the earth or in the air. Having killed him in the threshold of the palace, he did not die either inside or outside of a building.

Then, a curious thing happened. The creature was looking very closely inside of the demons body. Prahlada noticing this asked, "What are you looking for?"

Narsimha, with a gentle voice, answered, "Oh Prahlada, I am looking to see if there is another child like you in here."

The mysterious creature then offered the child a boon, and Prahlada asked that his father should attain a high state, and be freed from his sins. The Lord, being pleased the young devotee, fulfilled all his desires.

Praise and Abuse

Once an eager disciple went to his master for instructions. He asked the Guru what must he do to achieve Self-Realization. The Guru gave him an unusual instruction saying, "Go to the cemetery and swear at all the dead persons buried there in the name of their fathers, mothers, sisters and other relatives. Then return to me tomorrow."

The disciple did as he was instructed and returned to the Guru the next day.

This time the Guru instructed him saying, "Go to the cemetery again. Take perfumes and incense sticks with you. Light an incense stick on each grave and apply perfume to it. Then praise each dead person with all your heart, saying, "You are good, your father was good, your mother was good, and all your relatives are good." The disciple did exactly what he was told.

The next day the disciple returned to the Guru. When the master asked him what was the reaction of the dead when he praised and abused them the disciple said, "Guruji, what could they say, I praised and abused them but none of them heard."

The Guru answered, "You should become like them. Attain that state where honor and insult, praise and blame don't affect you, then you will achieve Self-Realization."

We should strive to attain equal vision, and become impervious to praise and blame. If a seeker cannot tolerate harsh words, what kind of seeker is he?

The Unfortunate Man

O nce, a man was traveling, and becoming tired he sat underneath a tree to rest. Now it so happened that this was no ordinary tree but a wish fulfilling tree.

Soon, the man started thinking how nice it would be if he had some delicious food to eat. Well, the moment he wished for it, the food suddenly appeared.

Next, he started thinking how nice it would be if he had a female companion there to enjoy the food with him. Just then a female appeared and she started making amorous eye gestures at him. They were soon enjoying each others company and he thought, "How nice it would be if we had a nice house to live in." The moment he thought of it, the house appeared.

He was now lying on a soft coach, enjoying the food and music from his new stereo system, along with his lady friend. But he started thinking about everything that had happened. He thought to himself, "I thought of food and it appeared, I thought of a companion and she appeared, then I thought of a house, that also appeared." All of a sudden he became frightened and thought, "Oh, there must be a demon here and this is his work," as he thought that, a demon suddenly appeared. The poor man saw the demon and thought, "He's going to eat me," and indeed, the demon ate him.

We should be careful about what we think. We are all sitting under a wish fulfilling tree, and the power of thought is great. Be happy and have good thoughts and give up worrying. Think of God and give up all delusions.

Duck Soup

Once someone gave Nasrudin a duck. He prepared some soup with it and shared it with the person. After they had finished the man left.

Later there was a knock on Nasrudin's door. "Who is there?" asked the *Mullah*.

"I'm a friend of the person who gave you the duck" came the answer.

Nasrudin let him in and offered him some of the duck soup, adding a little water to it. After the man had his fill he left.

After some time there was another knock on the door and Nasrudin asked, "Who is there?"

"I'm a friend of the friend of the man who gave you the duck," came the answer.

Nasrudin let him in and heated up the remaining soup, adding more water, since there was now only a little duck soup left, and offered it to the man. The man had his fill and left.

Again there was a knock on the door. "Who is it?," asked Nasrudin.

"I'm a friend of the friend of the friend of the man who gave you the duck," was the reply.

Nasrudin let the man in, but when he went to heat up the soup he found that there wasn't any left. So he poured some water into the pot, added salt and pepper and heated it, and offered that to the man. When the man tasted it he practically spit it out becoming very upset said, "What is this, this is not duck soup, it tastes like water. How can you offer this to me?"

Nasrudin tried to calm the man down and said, "My dear brother, be calm, what can I do, just as you are the friend of the friend of the friend of the man who gave me the duck, this is the soup of the soup of the soup of that original duck soup."

This was perhaps one of Baba's favorite stories. In the spiritual tradition it often occurs that the further one gets from the original master's message, the more watered down his teachings tend to become. After sometime the teachings and practices turn into an institutionalized religion, and instead of creating unity and harmony it creates divisiveness. Therefore, direct personal experience of divinity is very important. The original Master had a direct experience of the truth, but after sometime that truth is lost sight of by devotees.

You May Hiss, But Don't Bite

O nce there lived a terrible poisonous snake in a meadow near a village. The cobra was an expert in catching mice and frogs as well as warding off any intruders from his territory. He was a very big snake and the villagers were fearful of him. He was quick and could easily overtake a fleeing intruder, striking terror into their hearts. There was more then one villager who had perished as a result of his bite.

One day a *sadhu* happened to be traveling near the village and was heading towards the meadow. The villagers cautioned him saying, "Revered sir, please don't go that way. A venomous snake lives there and he will bite you."

The holy man said, "Don't worry, I know some *mantras* and the snake will not harm me," and he continued on his way. But the villagers were all afraid and did not accompany him.

Meanwhile, the snake had been sunning himself outside his hole when he became aware of a vibration in the earth, they were footsteps coming from the direction of the village. "Who dares intrude into my territory?" he thought. Thinking this way he coiled his body like a spring and raised his head spreading his hood. He began flicking his long tongue to taste the air and try to detect the intruder. He expected to sense fear and panic but to his astonishment this time he did not.

The sadhu came closer and closer until he was just about fifteen feet from the snake. All of a sudden the cobra shot forward ready to strike him. The sadhu immediately recited a secret mantra and the snake fell at his feet, listless.

The holy man said, "My dear brother, why do you go about do-ing harm?"

"I am simply trying to defend my territory," answered the snake, "as my ancestors have done for so long before me."

"By harming the villagers?" asked the sadhu, "by killing them?"

"Yes, of course," answered the snake. "How else is it to be done?"

"You should be ashamed," replied the sadhu. "You should stop biting people. Look, I will teach you a holy word. By repeating it you will learn to love God. Ultimately you will realize Him and also get rid of your violent nature. Try to control your negative impulses and repeat the mantra whenever you get the desire to strike anyone."

The holy man reached down and stroked the cobra's head with his hand, blessing him with the sacred mantra 'Om Namah Shivaya'.

The cobra felt a tremor move through his body at the sadhus touch and he bowed at his feet.

As the sadhu was about to leave he said, "I will go now my son, but I'll see you again."

The cobra began to sit at the base of a large hallowed out tree repeating the mantra with great love. Some weeks passed and the villagers noticed that the snake would not strike. Some of the village boys started harassing him by throwing stones at it. But still the snake showed no anger. One day one of the boys came close to it, caught it by the tail and started whirling him around and dashed him on the ground. The snake vomited blood and became unconscious. It could not move. The boys thought he was dead and so they left.

Late at night the snake regained consciousness. With great diffi-culty it dragged itself into its hole, but it could scarcely move, his body badly bruised. Many days passed. The snake became a mere skeleton covered with skin. Every once in a while it came out at night in search of food. Do to the fear of the boys it would not leave its hole during the day time. Since receiving the sacred mantra he had given up eating mice and frogs and maintained his life on leaves, roots and fruits that had dropped naturally from the trees.

Months passed in this way and as the cobra became a vegetarian the mice population also grew. The villagers tried to deal with it the best they could, but it was not easy. Their grain bins were being diminished very quickly.

About a year later the sadhu came that way again. He went to the meadow where the cobra lived and started searching for his disciple calling it by the name he had given him. Hearing the Guru's voice the snake came out of its hole and bowed before him with great reverence.

"How are you?" asked the sadhu.

"I am well," replied the snake.

"But why are you so thin," asked the concerned teacher.

The snake replied, "Guruji, you ordered me not to harm anybody. So I have been living only on roots, leaves and fruit. Perhaps that has made me thinner."

The snake had totally forgotten that the village boys had been harassing him and had almost killed him.

The sadhu said, "It can't be mere want of food which has reduced you to such a state, look at your tattered body. There must be some other reason. Think carefully and try to remember."

As he thought back the snake said, "Well, yes Guruji, there is something else," and he recounted how the village boys harassed him and even tried to kill him. The snake said, "They are ignorant, after all. They didn't realize what a great change had come over my mind. Since you instructed me not to bite anyone I have been following your command."

The sadhu said sternly, "How foolish you are! You let them nearly kill you? Did I tell you to let yourself become defenseless? You don't know how to protect yourself."

The cobra said, "But sir, I thought..."

"You thought!" questioned the sadhu before the snake could finish, "Unfortunately you did not think."

"I have tried to follow your instructions," said the cobra. "You told me not to strike the village boys, nor to chase them. You said to harm no one."

"I told you not to strike them; but did I tell you not to hiss at them?" asked the sadhu.

The cobra was silent.

"My son," the sadhu went on, "you must be strong. I did not ask you to give up your usual means of livelihood. You have your own part to play in the great dance of life. Giving up mice and frogs creates an imbalance in nature and you are therefore not performing your duties."

The cobra said, "I have failed in your instructions Oh Guruji."

"Now, now," the sadhu said consolingly. "You have not failed, I should have made myself more clear. In any case just think of this past year as a time of great austerities. You have done very well." "But remember," the sadhu continued, "if you are ever molested by the village boys, do not hesitate to hiss ferociously at them. But never inject your venom into them."

St. Augustine's Dream

Saint Augustine, after many years of study and searching, found no inner contentment. He wanted to know God so badly that he became like a mad man.

One night, he had a dream in which he was walking along the seashore. At a short distance he saw a small child standing near the water. The child had a small cup in his hand and there was an intense troubled expression on his face. When Augustine got closer he asked the child what the matter was. The child told him that he was trying to scoop up the ocean with his cup. Augustine laughed and said, "my child, you will never be able to scoop up the whole ocean with your little cup."

The child looked at Augustine and asked, "How is what I am trying to do different then what you are trying to do, aren't you also attempting to scoop up God with your little cup?" The child then said, "But, I will show you how it can be done," and he threw the cup into the ocean. Augustine immediately understood its implication and tears of joy arose in him.

We should not try to hold God within our small cups, but we ourselves should merge completely into him.

The Monk and the Woman

Once, a monk heard of a great master and decided to go and spend some time with him. After sometime the master decided to go on a pilgrimage and asked the novice monk to accompany him.

After walking for awhile they came to a river. At the banks of the river a woman was standing trying to get across, but the river was too deep for her.

Without hesitation the older monk put her on his back and carried her across. Setting her down on the other side they continued on their way.

After sometime, unable to contain himself any longer, the novice monk said to the master, "How could you do that, don't you know that monks are not allowed to touch woman? Have you forgotten your vows? It is not right for you to act so improper."

This went on for about an hour until finally the older monk said, "Calm yourself brother, I have already put down that woman at the river bank, but why do you continue to carry her?"

Fault-finding and criticizing others gives rise to self-delusion. Therefore, look on everyone with compassion and understanding.

All is God

There lived a holy man in the forest who had many disciples. One day he taught them to see God in all beings, and knowing this, to bow low before them all.

One day, one of his disciples went to the forest to gather wood for the sacrificial fire. Suddenly he heard an outcry, "Get out of the way! A mad elephant is coming!"

Everyone but the disciple of the holy man ran off. He reasoned that the elephant was also God in another form. Then why should he run away from it? He stood still, bowed before the raging animal, and began to sing its praises. The elephant's *mahout* was shouting, "Get out of the way! Run away!"

But the disciple didn't move. The animal suddenly seized him with his trunk, cast him to one side, and went on his way. Hurt and bruised, the disciple lay unconscious on the ground. Hearing what had happened his teacher and brother disciples came to him and carried him back to the hermitage. The Guru administered some medicine and the disciple regained consciousness. Someone asked him, "You knew the elephant was coming, so why didn't you move out of the way?"

"But," he answered, "our teacher has taught us that God Himself has taken all these forms, of animals as well as men. Therefore, thinking it was only the elephant God that was coming, I didn't run away."

The teacher said, "Yes my child, it is true that the elephant God was coming, but why did you not listen to the mahout God, who was shouting at you to move out of the way?"

It is not enough to just hear spiritual teachings. Their meanings must be reflected and meditated upon. A similar incident once occurred to a seeker who had taken a weekend seminar given by my Guru. In that seminar Baba had also spoken on the same subject, 'the all pervasiveness of God', and how He had assumed all the various forms in the universe. During the break the seeker went out on the street for a walk and came across a dog. The person was warned that the dog may bite, but he insisted on petting him, remembering Baba's morning lecture. "All is God," he reasoned, "this dog will not harm me." Sure enough, the moment he got close to the dog, the dog bit him. After seeing a doctor the boy returned to the seminar. During the question and answer period the boy asked Baba what had gone wrong? He said when he approached the dog he believed Baba's teaching that he was God and so was the dog. Baba answered, "Why does this surprise you, after all, you took the seminar, but the dog did not."

Nasrudin and the Buffalo

Nasrudin used to enjoy sitting out on his porch. His neighbor owned a large water buffalo and Nasrudin had a strong desire to ride him. He used to sit there picturing himself riding on the head of the buffalo, right in between his large horns. He was always thinking about how to accomplish this. This went on for many months. Finally one day, as he was sitting on the porch, the buffalo came right into his front yard and sat down. Nasrudin was ecstatic, and thought this was an opportunity sent by God.

He immediately jumped up and ran over to the buffalo and sat on his head right in between his horns, just as he had imagined himself doing all those months. The moment he sat down the buffalo got up and shook his head violently throwing Nasrudin flat on his back. The Mullah was in great pain, and thought that he had broken his back. His wife heard the commotion and ran out to see what was going on. She found Nasrudin lying on his back and ran to him asking what had happened.

He told her how he had tried to ride the buffalo and was thrown to the ground. His wife asked, "My dear husband, what are you doing, you should have thought about this before attempting such a crazy idea."

"What are you saying," Nasrudin shot back, "don't you know that I have been thinking about this for many months?"

Like Nasrudin, we often think about many things. But the real question is, what are we thinking about? Do we think about the right things? We should understand the nature of the mind, and examine our thoughts carefully. Discrimination is very important for happiness.

The Blind Men

There were some blind men who had the habit of sitting at a local tea shop talking to each other while having tea. One day an unusual event took place. An Elephant, with his *mahout* riding on his back came near the shop. The blind men heard the commotion and also heard the huge bell around the Elephants neck that rang as he walked. When the Elephant came nearer some of the blind men started to feel different parts of the animal. One felt the Elephants ear, and as he did so the Elephant fanned them. Feeling the breeze, the man said, "An Elephant is like a large hand fan."

One of the others, who was feeling one of the legs, and putting his arms around it said, "No, no, it is like a pillar which holds up a palace."

Another had gotten a hold of the Elephants trunk and as soon as the Elephant curled it to smell him he dropped it saying, "What are you saying, are you all mad, it is like a serpent, stay away from it."

Another had grabbed the tail and thinking it felt fibrous with its tough hairs said, "No, you are all wrong, it is just like a rope."

In this way an argument flared up amongst themselves. Finally, the mahout called out to them and said, "Brothers, why do you argue like this. the Elephant is like all you have stated and more. The elephant is not a pillar, its legs are like pillars. It is not a fan but its ears are like fans. It is not a snake but its trunk is like a snake. It is not a rope but its tale is like a rope. Due to your blindness you are not able to see the whole animal. In order to get a

28

better idea of what the Elephant is really like, you should try to imagine a creature with all of those ideas combined.

This is perhaps one of the oldest stories told by many great masters to convey the limited power of humanity when trying to convey that which is limitless. God is like that elephant, and everyone else like those blind men. Some see one part, while others view another, and then think they have seen the whole elephant. From this limited perception conflicts arise, and one believes that their religious beliefs are superior to another.

The Lord and His Horse

There was once a very rich shepherd and he owned a large herd of sheep and goats. He was also a great devotee of God and worshipped him in a personal form, in the form known as *Khandoba*, God sitting on a horse. Since he was wealthy, he had the images made of gold.

Now as time passed the shepherd ran into some bad luck. He lost all of his wealth and everything he owned. He barely had enough food to eat. One day a friend went to him and said, "Ramja, you've become very poor. You require some capital to start up your business again. Why don't you sell the images of your God and his horse. That way you can purchase more sheep and goats and when you get back on your feet, you can again have new images made.

At first Ramja did not like this idea, but he knew it was the only way to get started again. He took the images into town to sell. He went to a goldsmith and showed the images to him, saying, "Sir, I have brought my Lord and his horse to sell."

The goldsmith said fine and proceeded to weigh them individually. He first weighed the Lord's image and it weighed a pound and a half. "I'll give you two thousand dollars for this," said the goldsmith.

The goldsmith next weighed the horse, that came to three pounds. "For this one I'll give you four thousand dollars," he said.

When Ramja heard this, he became very angry. "You are a fool," he shouted, "You value the horse more then my Lord? How is that possible, don't you have any sense?"

The goldsmith tried to calm Ramja down, saying, "Ramja, calm yourself, I'm buying gold, I'm not interested in your Lord or his horse. I don't care about that. You may call one your Lord and the other his horse, but for me they are just gold."

In this way, all that exists is that One Consciousness. Like that goldsmith, we should perceive the great Spirit pervading everything. Sorrow arises when we do not see the unity in diversity.

Dipping It In Water, Rubbing It On A Stone

Shivaji, the great seventeenth century Maharastrian king, had invited his Guru, Samartha Ramdass to come and bless his palace. Even though Ramdass had been invited on numerous occasions he had kept putting it off. Finally, one day Ramdass had the impulse to visit the capital and he started walking in that direction. It had been raining quite heavily and all the ponds were full of water. On the way Ramdass noticed a bull eyeing him while sporting happily in one of the ponds. The bull would rub his horns in the mud, then dip them in water, and then rubbed them on a stone. Smiling and absorbed in ecstasy, Ramdass said to himself, "Yes, dipping it in water, rubbing it against the stone, I know what's in your mind."

As he continued on his journey to the capital he kept repeating this as if it were a mantra.

When Ramdass reached the palace Shivaji received him with great honor. He stayed in the palace for a few weeks and then left. But before he left Shivaji asked him to bless him with a mantra. Ramdass, still absorbed in the words he had been repeating said, "Dipping it in water, rubbing it against the stone, I know what's in your mind," and left the palace.

Shivaji had full faith in his Guru and took this statement as his Guru's mantra initiation and started repeating it always.

One day the king went to his barber for his regular shave. Now it so happened that the barber had been hired by the kings enemies to cut his throat while he was giving him a shave.

The king sat in the chair, closed his eyes and started repeating his new mantra aloud, "Dipping it in water, rubbing it against a stone, I know what's in your mind."

The barber was sharpening his razor by dipping it in water and then rubbing it on a stone, and when he heard what the king said he just about fainted, thinking that the king had found him out. He fell at the kings feet and confessed the plot, and begged for his forgiveness. The king was amazed at this, but he forgave the barber and threw the conspirators in prison.

Even the seemingly unimportant utterings of a saint has great power. Whatever words come from the Guru's lips has great authority, and those words will always bless and protect a devoted disciple in some way.

When God Laughs

It is said that God laughs on two occasions. He laughs when the physician says to the patient's mother, "Don't be afraid mother, I shall certainly cure your child."

God laughs saying to Himself, "I am going to take this life and this man says he will save it!" The physician thinks he is the master, forgetting that God is the master.

God laughs again when two brothers divide their land with a string saying to each other, "This side is mine, and that side is yours." He laughs and says to Himself, "The universe belongs to Me, but these foolish brothers say they own this portion or that portion!"

Gajendra
The King of Elephants

Once upon a time there lived an elephant called Gajendra. He was called Gajendra because he was the king of elephants. He was so powerful that even at his scent other elephants, lions, tigers, and other carnivorous animals took flight through sheer terror.

One day Gajendra, while in the company of a herd of elephants, entered a beautiful forest garden. He was in a state of intoxication and was going about breaking and treading down trees and shrubs. Being oppressed by the heat of the Sun, he headed towards a nearby lake which was full with lotus flowers.

Plunging into the lake, he, with the tip of his trunk, started drinking the cool water perfumed with the pollen of golden and blue lotuses. Bathing himself in the waters of the lake, he became refreshed.

The proud, yet compassionate elephant, let his female mates and their young calves drink the water and bathe, spraying them with the cool water. In this way he was lost in sporting with his mates.

Suddenly, a powerful crocodile caught hold of Gajendra's leg. Realizing he was caught, the mighty elephant exerted himself will all his might to free himself from the animal's jaws. But the crocodile continued to pull him into the lake.

Noticing that their leader was being dragged with such force, the female elephants simply began to shriek. The other elephants came to his aid but, though helping him from behind and sides, they were unable to free him.

The struggle went on for many days. The elephant tried to drag the crocodile outside the water, while the crocodile was pulling him back inside. In this way, due to the long and intense struggle, the king of elephants became very weak, while the reverse appeared to be true for the aquatic crocodile.

As the other elephants saw that they too were being dragged into the lake, they thought, "Why should we also loose our lives? It is better that only one member of our group is lost." Thinking in this manner one by one they all left poor Gajendra to his fate. His wife left him, his children left him, all his relatives left him. As Gajendra looked back, he saw no one there to help him. "Alas," he thought, "my life has come to an end. Everyone has abandoned me, even after all I have done for them. Caught up as I am in the snare of destiny in the form of this crocodile, I shall now approach the Supreme Lord who is the last refuge of all."

Saying this, he plucked a lotus flower with his trunk and throwing it into the air as an offering to the Lord, said, "Oh Lord, I am dying, please except this flower on my behalf."

The moment he made this gesture of self surrender there was a loud thunder and a lighting bolt struck the crocodile, resulting in the instantaneous freedom of Gajendra. In order to show that it is never to late to call on the Lord the poet says, "Even though Gajendra remembered the Lord only at the end, due to God's compassion he saved him from the jaws of death."

The Pundit Who Could Not Swim

Once several men were crossing the river *Ganga* in a boat. One of them, a *pundit*, was making a great display of his scholarship, saying how he had studied various scriptures like the Vedas, the Vedanta, and the other systems of Philosophy.

He then turned to the boatman and asked, "Do you know the Vedanta?"

"No, revered sir," the boatman replied.

"Have you studied grammar or the Yoga sutras?"

"No, revered sir."

"Have you read any Philosophy whatsoever?" inquired the pundit.

"No, revered sir," answered the boatman

The pundit then said, "Well, half of your life has been lost."

Soon a storm arose and the boat was about to sink. The boatman said to the pundit, "Sir, can you swim?"

"No" replied the pundit.

"In that case," said the boatman, "your whole life is lost!"

What will a person gain from empty knowledge of the scriptures? One must know how to cross the river of life.

Appearances Are Deceiving

Once Mullah Nasrudin was riding his donkey and came across the king's hunting party. Now, to see someone with an unusual face the first thing in the morning was considered bad luck, and was believed to spoil the whole day. So, when the King noticed Nasrudin he thought, "How unusual that man looks, and he is also riding a donkey. This cannot be a good omen for the hunt," and he ordered that Nasrudin be taken and put into prison. Poor Nasrudin, he was beaten by the king's guards and thrown into prison.

But as it turned out, the king actually had a very successful day and he caught many animals. He started to rethink about Nasrudin and ordered his men to bring him from the dungeon. When Nasrudin arrived the king said, "Oh Mullah, when I saw your unusual appearance I thought that you were a bad omen for me, but as you can see I have caught a lot of game and so in fact you must have been auspicious for me." The Mullah replied, "Oh King, it seems that you are right, that in seeing my face this good fortune has befalling you, but your majesty, I can not say the same about you. When I saw your face it proved very inauspicious for me. So, who is a bad omen, and who is a good omen?"

Therefore, one should never judge an individual by their appearance alone. Instead, we should look at everyone with the awareness of equality.

The Monkey and the Tiger

Once there was an old tiger. When the tiger was young he used to terrorize all the other animals. But as he grew old he had become very weak and was unable to catch any animals for his food. The tiger thought to himself, "What shall I do? Now that I'm old I can't catch anything to eat and no one will come near me."

Thinking in this way, he came upon a plan. He decided to become a sadhu, a holy tiger. He went ahead and put on the robes of a monk and wherever he walked, he would move very slowly, blowing away any little insect from under his feet, so as not to harm them.

One day, a monkey saw the tiger coming in his direction. The monkey was about to run away, since he knew that tigers ate monkeys, but he noticed that the tiger was walking very slowly and as he took each step he would gently blow away any creature that were underfoot. The monkey was intrigued at what he saw. He thought, "Could this really be a non-violent tiger?"

The tiger came a bit closer repeating the holy mantra: "Om Shanti! Shanti! Shanti!," and he then sat down, cleaning the area gently of any creatures that maybe harmed.

He started speaking to the monkey saying, "Don't be afraid my child, I have given up my past evil actions and have been initiated into a religious order that practices non-violence. I now practice penance in order to expedite my past sins."

"How has this change come about?," asked the monkey.

The tiger answered, "My dear brother, when I looked back on my life, I became filled with remorse. I misled so many creatures by teaching them the path of violence that I decided to turn my life around, and so I took initiation into the path of non-violence."

The monkey was now convinced that he had truly found a great being. He thought finally, "I have met a great Guru who is absorbed in his own inner Self." Hoping to get some instructions from him, he moved very close to the tiger and bowed his head. But the moment he did so, the tiger grabbed him by the throat.

The poor monkey now realized that he had been duped and he thought for sure his end had come. He thought, "What a fool I have been, this tiger has deceived me with his pose of peace and non-violence."

He thought and thought about what he should do to escape, and then suddenly he had an idea. Even though he was terrified, he started laughing out loud saying, "Ho ho ho ho, ha ha ha ha, how wonderful! how wonderful!"

The tiger was puzzled at this behavior and asked the monkey, "Why are you laughing and shouting, `How wonderful, how wonderful?', you should be frightened, yet you are laughing."

The monkey said, "Oh tiger, I know the science of astrology, and I have come to know that whoever dies at this very moment will automatically go to heaven. So, as you can see, I am very happy about dying."

The tiger himself did not want to miss this opportunity and he let go of the monkey for a moment to think about how he too could die. But the moment he let go, the monkey immediately ran up a tree, and started crying and praying, "Oh Lord, Oh Lord."

The tiger, watching from below said, "What is this? While you were in my clutches you laughed when you should have been crying; now that you are free, you are crying when you should be laughing?"

The monkey replied, "Oh tiger, first I laughed to escape your clutches, but now I am crying to God for having given birth to deceivers like you. I'm praying that he stops sending such cheats dressed as teachers."

One should recognize a true Guru. Discrimination is needed when seeking out a teacher. It is a tradition that Guru's test seekers for a long time before accepting them as disciples. In the same way, a seeker should test the Guru. The seeker should keep the company of a Guru long enough to know his habits and see what changes occur within himself.

The Country Club

Once a group of religious people purchased a piece of land to build a temple on. When the temple was finished they consecrated it to Vishnu, hoping that many people would come to worship there. But, as it turned out, only a few devotees of Vishnu came.

After waiting in vain for more worshippers to attend, the trustees decided to change the deity of the temple from Vishnu to Shiva.

Now, a few of the followers of Shiva started coming, but the followers of Vishnu stopped coming. In fact, they were upset about the change and marched in protest outside the temple.

Since there were so few people coming, the trustees held a meeting and decided to change the building completely. They said, "All right, instead of a Hindu temple, well build a mosque instead."

So, they tore down the temple and built a mosque. Naturally, all the Hindus stopped coming. Some Muslims came, but only on Fridays, the Muslim holy day.

The trustees decided that too few people were coming and thought a Synagogue would attract more people. So the mosque was torn down and a Jewish temple was built in its place. Of course all Muslims stopped coming, but the few Jews who came also came only one day a week, on Saturday, their holy day.

The trustees met again trying to figure out how to get more people to come. They said, "Perhaps if we build a church more people will come. After all, there are many Christians." So, once again they tore down the existing building and built a magnificent church. Now, a few more people came but still there weren't very many, and those came only on Sunday, the Christian holy day.

By this time the trustees were thoroughly disgusted. They said, "These religions don't seem to work at all. People are so preoccupied with religious differences that one faith negates another. In fact, they seem to only cause problems." So, they took a vote and decided to tear down the church and build a hotel with a nightclub, tennis court, swimming pool and other facilities. Soon everybody started coming, Hindus, Muslims, Jews, Christians and people of other faiths. They did not limit their visits to any particular days of the week but came every day of the week.

Even though the founders of the different religions meant to bring everyone together, still, their followers, lacking the vision of unity, have created a sense of separation. The truth is that God is not the exclusive property of any particular religion.

Heaven Becomes Hell

Once, someone asked my Guru a question. They said, "Muslims say that Allah is the only God, Christians say that one must follow only Jesus to be saved, and the Hare Krishna's say that their way is the only way. All religions seem to say the same thing, that anyone who doesn't follow us will go to hell. What do you say about this?"

Baba answered, "Don't be afraid of hell. All these Mullahs, priests and others are always cursing scientists, engineers, architects, and those with other talents. They said, "All those people have corrupted our religion, so they will go to hell!" And they did go to hell. However, when they looked at hell they said, "This is a terrible place!" But they were very talented, and when they saw how bad the place was, they began to improve it. They began to change the plumbing system, and the drainage system, and they also planted beautiful gardens. Soon they began building apartments, hotels, country clubs and movie theaters. Everything became first class. And when they had changed the drainage system, all the waste matter that had been flowing down to hell began to flow to heaven!"

"So," continued Baba, "now you don't have to worry about hell, because it has become heaven. Let the priests go to their heaven. We will enjoy our own beautiful new country, and we will live there very happily. And if there are people who say, 'We want to go to heaven,' then I will tell them, 'You should just meditate and give up all religions, because ultimately these religions will take you only to their own heaven, which has now become hell.'"

The Story of Dhruva
The Pole Star

O nce, there lived a king named Uttanapada. He had two wives named Suruci and Suniti. The king had a son by each of them.

One day, while the king was fondling Suruci's son Uttama on his lap, Dhruva, the son of Suniti also tried to climb up on his lap. But the king refused and his stepmother, Suruci, out of jealousy for her own son said to Dhruva, "Oh child, even though you are the king's son, you do not deserve to ascend the royal throne, since you were not born as my child."

Being criticized by his stepmother with such harsh words, the young child ran to his mother crying. She embraced him and lifted him up on her lap trying to calm him. She said to him, "Oh child! Remain above jealousy. Abide by the true path. If you desire the highest throne, then propitiate the feet of Lord Vishnu, who is the father of all. Adore him by focusing your mind exclusively on him. He is the only one who can remedy your grievances."

Even though Dhruva was only a child of five years of age, he took this advice of his mother to heart and left the palace in search of the Lord.

While wandering about, Dhruva came across the celestial sage Narada. Narada asked, "Oh child, where are you going alone, leaving behind your home which is full of prosperity? I can perceive that you are upset about something."

Dhruva related his sad tale and said that he was in search of his real father, Lord Vishnu.

In order to test his resolve, Narada pointed out that this was indeed a difficult task and many have tried and failed. Therefore the sage said, "Return to your home and enjoy the worldly life. Perhaps when you are older you may think about this again."

But Dhruva was not to be deterred so easily. He answered Narada by saying, "Oh Narada! Out of compassion you have shown the true path to others and guided them to its fulfillment. I desire to secure a place which is the highest and most exalted of all the worlds, and which has never been attained by anyone else. Be pleased to show me the proper path to achieve it."

Narada was very pleased to hear the child's response. Placing his hand on the boys head and blessing him with a mantra, he told him to go to the banks of the river Yamuna to practice his meditation.

Dhruva did as he was told by the sage and started practicing intense austerities, and breath control. He meditated for long hours and fasted for many days at a time.

In this way many months passed and his mind became focused in his heart, meditating on the form of the Lord described to him by Narada. He meditated on the Lord, who is the Soul of the universe as not being different from himself. He soon started to experience great joy and inner peace.

Finally, the Lord being pleased with him, appeared before Dhruva. Awed at his presence, the child bowed to him, bending down his body and prostrating himself before him on the ground like a stick. Dhruva then praised the Lord with a hymn which spontaneously arose from an inner inspiration.

After the hymn, the Lord spoke to Dhruva saying, "Oh young prince, I know what you cherish in your heart. You have observed your vows with strict discipline. I will bestow on you your cherished object even though it is unattainable by others. I confer on you that resplendent eternal place on which is based the entire circle of stellar luminaries, like the planets and constellations of stars. Your position will be like a central post around which the circle of luminous bodies are fastened."

After saying this, Dhruva, the child devotee, became known as the pole star. Looking up at the midnight sky we can see him as the central star in which all others revolve.

The Loincloth

A sadhu, under the instructions of his Guru, built himself a small hut away from the townspeople. He soon began his spiritual practices in his hut. Now, every morning after his bath in the river he would hang his loincloth on a tree next to his hut. One day, on his return from begging his food from a nearby village, he found that rats had chewed holes in his loincloth. So the next day he had to go to the local village for a new one. A few days later, the sadhu spread his new loincloth on the roof of his hut to dry and went to beg for his food. On his return he found that the rats had chewed the cloth into shreds. The sadhu was very annoyed thinking, "What will I do, I can't keep begging for new loincloths all the time?" In any case, he went into the village the next day and told the villagers what had happened. The villagers said, "Who will keep given you loincloths every day? You should do one thing, get a cat, it will keep away the rats."

The sadhu thought that was a good idea and got a kitten in the village and took it back to his hut. From that day the rats ceased to trouble him. He was very happy. The sadhu now began to care for the kitten and started to feed it milk which he begged from the village.

After about a week, a villager said to him, "Swamiji, you require milk every day. You can get your milk by begging, but how long will people keep supplying you with milk? You should do one thing - keep a cow. You then can satisfy your own needs as well as the cats."

In a few days the sadhu procured a cow and thereby did not have to beg for milk any more. But, within a short time he found that he had to beg for straw for his cow. He had to visit the neighboring villagers for the straw, but the villagers said, "There are lots of uncultivated lands close to your hut, just cultivate the land and you won't have to beg for straw anymore." The sadhu took their advice and started tilling the land. Gradually he had to engage some laborers and later on found it necessary to build a barn to store the crop. In this way he became a sort of landlord. Eventually he took a wife to help him look after his large household and they also had children, and so had to build a large house. He now passed his days like a busy householder.

After some years passed his Guru came to see him. Finding a number of buildings and goods, the Guru was puzzled and inquired of a servant, "An ascetic used to live here in a hut, can you tell me where he has moved to?" The servant did not know what to say. So the Guru went inside the house, where he met his disciple. The Guru said to him, "My son, what is all this?" The disciple, in great shame, fell at the Guru's feet and said, "Oh Gurudev, all for a single loincloth!"

Very Well, Very Well

Once, there was a girl in a fishing village who had become an unwed mother. After several beatings from her father she finally revealed who the father of the child was. She said it was the Zen master living on the outskirts of the village.

The villagers marched to the masters house, rudely disturbing his meditation, denounced him as a hypocrite, and told him to keep the baby.

All the master said was, "Very well. Very well."

The master picked up the baby and made arrangements for a woman from the village to feed, clothe and look after the child at his own expense. Of course the master's name was ruined and his disciples all abandoned him.

After this had gone on for about a year, the girl who had borne the child could not stand it any longer and she finally confessed that she had lied. The father of the child was not the master but the boy next door.

The villagers were all very upset when they heard this. They went to the master's house and prostrated themselves at his feet and begged his pardon, and asked for the child back. The master returned the child, saying only, "Very well. Very well."

This is the state of a realized being. They accept whatever comes their way, good or bad, without any fuss.

Sheik Shibli and The Two Seekers

Two men once went to the great sufi master Sheik Shibli to ask for initiation. Shibli at once saw that one of them was deserving and the other was not. He therefore asked them to come to him separately, since each would have to be dealt with differently.

When the first man came, Shibli asked him to recite a mantra.

The man said, "Please tell me exactly what you would like me to say."

Shibli told him, "God is one, There is none except Him, and Shibli is His prophet."

When the man heard this he exclaimed, "Why, it is perfectly clear to see that you are nothing but a common *fakir*, like hundreds of others who have no special merit. Yet you claim to be the Holy Prophet of God Himself."

Sheik Shibli said, "My friend, I do not believe you should have come to me. It will be much better for you to go to a Mullah in some mosque."

When the second man came, Shibli again repeated, "God is one, There is non except Him, and Shibli is His prophet."

"Oh, what a great pity that is," said the man, with a sigh of disappointment. "I am a good Muslim and have studied the Koran, and it tells us of Mohammed and other great prophets of God. If you are only a prophet, then I have no need of you, for I am already a follower of the Prophet."

"Oh brother, what was it then that you were seeking?," asked Shibli.

"I was searching for a true Fakir, one who is one with God Himself," answered the man. "I have heard that there were such God-men, and that they could give their disciples an experience of unity with the Lord. Many people told me that you were such a one, but it now turns out that you are nothing more then a prophet."

The man turned to go, but Shibli, throwing his arms around him and embracing him warmly said, "Brother, you are indeed the deserving one. You are a true lover of God. Have no doubts or fears, for, it will be a great joy to give you the gift of initiation."

Don't Imitate The Guru

Once there lived a great being named Makarios. He lived a simple life and had a number of disciples. One day he was sitting with his disciples on the bank of a lake giving a lecture. While he was talking, he would stick his hand into the water, pull out some fishes, and swallow them live.

Now Makarios had been teaching and following a vegetarian diet but when the disciples saw this action of the Guru, they thought, perhaps a non-vegetarian diet is good. So they caught a lot of fish, cooked them, adding some spices, and ate their fill, washing them down with plenty of wine. Makarios remained silent.

Later the group moved on, and the disciples felt happy to be with such a wonderful master.

After awhile they stopped on the banks of another lake and saint Makarios sat down. All of sudden, he spat out the fish he had swallowed at the previous lake. They were all alive, and they began to swim about in the water.

"Now spit out your fishes," Makarios said to his disciples. The disciples tried, but of course they were not able to.

Saint Makarios said, "There were no fishes in this lake, so I have brought some from that other lake, which had an abundant amount."

We should follow the path shown by the Guru, and practice his teachings not imitate his ways. Otherwise, we will make many mistakes. Often seekers start imitating the Guru's outer mannerisms without paying attention to his inner state.

The Un-Accepted Gift

Once a man went to see Buddha and he started to abuse him, but Buddha kept silent. Finally, the man became frustrated and asked him why he didn't answer.

The Buddha asked him, "If a man declined to accept a gift, to whom did it return to?"

The man answered, "Why, to the person who gave it of course."

The Buddha said, "I don't accept your gift of abuses."

The Buddha took this opportunity to teach his disciples and said that when a wicked man abuses a virtuous person, it is like one who looks up and spits at heaven. Heaven does not get soiled, but the spittle will only fall back on him!

The Secret of the Locked Room

The pious Ayaz was originally brought to the court of Mahmud, the monarch of Ghazna, as a slave. But Mahmud became fond of him and eventually made him his adviser and friend.

Unfortunately, the other courtiers were jealous of Ayaz, and observed his every move, hoping to catch him at some shortcoming and thereby denounce him to the king.

One day, they went to Mahmud and said, "Oh great monarch! You should know that due to our loyalty to you, we have been keeping an eye on your slave Ayaz. We wish to report to you that every day when he leaves the court, he goes into a small room where nobody else is ever allowed. He spends some time there and then goes to his own quarters. We are afraid that this habit of his is somehow connected with a guilty secret, perhaps even consorting with plotters against your life."

Now Mahmud had for a long time refused to hear anything against Ayaz. But the mystery of the locked room intrigued even him and he felt he had to question Ayaz.

One day, when Ayaz was coming out of his room, Mahmud, surrounded by his ministers appeared and demanded to be shown the room.

"No," said Ayaz.

"If you do not allow me to enter the room," said the king, "all my confidence and trust in your loyalty will disappear." "Take your choice," the fierce conqueror said.

Ayaz wept, but threw open the door of the room and allowed Mahmud to enter. The room was empty of all furniture. The only thing it contained was a staff, a begging-bowl and a tattered and patched cloak hanging on a hook on the wall.

The king and his staff were unable to understand the significance of this discovery and Mahmud demanded an explanation.

Ayaz said, "Mahmud, for years I have been your slave, your friend and counselor. But I have tried to never forget my origins and for this reason I have come here every day to remind myself of what I was. I belong to you, and all that belongs to me is my rags, my stick, my begging-bowl, and my wanderings over the earth."

First Learn The Scriptures Well

A learned brahmin once went to a wise king and proclaimed, "Oh King, I am well versed in the holy scriptures, and I intend to teach you the Bhagavata."

The king, who was the wiser of the two, knew that a man who had really studied the Bhagavata Purana would seek to know his own Self rather then go to a king's court for wealth and honor. So the king replied, "I see, Oh brahmana, that you yourself have not as yet mastered that book thoroughly. I promise to make you my tutor, but first learn the scripture well."

The brahmin returned home thinking, "How foolish that king is to say that I have not mastered the Bhagavata, seeing that I have been reading it over and over all these years." However, he went through the book carefully once more and again went to see the king. The king told him the same thing and sent him away. The brahmin was very puzzled, but thought that there must be some meaning in the kings behavior. He went home, shut himself in his room and applied himself more then ever to the study of the book. He started meditating deeply on it and soon, hidden meanings began to flash into his mind. He realized the vanity of running after riches and honor, kings and courts, wealth and fame. From then onwards he gave himself up entirely to attaining perfection by worshipping God, and never again thought of returning to the king.

A few years later, the king thought of the brahmin and went to his house to see what he was doing. Seeing him, now radiant with a divine inner light, he fell to his knees and said, "I see that you have now realized the true meaning of the scriptures. I am ready to be your disciple if you will kindly accept me."

Satyakama Jabala

Once, young Satyakama asked his mother, "Oh Mother, what is my lineage? I wish to go and study with a Guru and he will want to know my parentage."

The child did not realize that this would be an embarrassing question for his mother, but she composed herself and replied, "My child, to tell you the truth I do not know who your father is. You were conceived when I was young and wandering as a housemaid serving here and there. But I know one thing, and that is that your name is Satyakama, and my name is Jabala. Therefore, say to your Guru that you are Satyakama Jabala."

The son agreed and said good-bye to his mother. He went in search of a teacher who would accept him as a student. He approached the teacher Haridrumata Gautama who was known for his wisdom. After bowing to him, Satyakama asked the teacher to accept him as his student.

"My boy, what is your family lineage?" asked the sage.

Satyakama replied, "Sir, as I started on this journey I asked my mother this very question." Saying that, the boy narrated the exact words spoken to him by his mother. He then said, "I am therefore known as Satyakama Jabala."

The Guru, perceiving the honesty of the boy said, "My child, you are indeed brave and truthful. No one not born of a brahmin would relate such an unpleasant truth. Therefore I accept you as my pupil. Now go and get fuel for the sacrificial fire so that I may initiate you into the life of *bramacharya*."

After performing the initiation the Guru gave Satyakama four hundred lean and sickly cattle, saying, "My child, take good care of these and return to me when they have multiplied to one thousand."

The boy drove the cattle to the forest and vowed that he would not return until they were a herd of one thousand. He lived in the forest for many years looking after the cattle with great devotion. Even though the boy was not given any formal teachings, a change started to occur in him. He started to become very sensitive to his environment, and as he sat quietly meditating, he felt a deep inner peace. It soon appeared to him that all creation was a manifestation of God. The sun, the moon, the stars, the forest and the creatures residing there, all these were manifestations of the Lord. As he looked at the gentle cows, they too were divine and he felt a subtle communion with them. The four cardinal directions were also part of the Lord. In fact, wherever he looked he saw only that divinity. At night, when he sat in front of the fire, it appeared that it spoke to him. His mind slowly realized the inner Self in his breath, in touch, in sight, in hearing, in speech, and in taste. Even the different creatures appeared to reveal knowledge of nature to him.

Finally one day, when the herd had become one thousand, the bull of the herd approached him and said, "Satyakama, we have become a herd of one thousand. Take us back to your Guru's ashram."

They started back to the ashram and on the way Satyakama reflected on the years he had spent in the forest. Everything appeared very clear to him now and as he got closer to the ashram his experiences became crystallized.

When he arrived at the ashram his Guru was very pleased to see him. Satyakama bowed to him and his Guru asked, "My son, your face shines like one who has known Brahman. Who was it that taught you?"

"By beings other then men," replied Satyakama. "But I desire that you should teach me. For I have heard from the wise that the knowledge imparted from the Guru will lead to the supreme good."

The Guru knew that the disciple was ripe, and was then ready to receive spiritual knowledge. He therefore blessed him with his touch and imparted to Satyakama the highest truth. This story was first narrated in the Chandogya Upanishad.

Whatever Happens Is For The Best

Birbal, a wise brahmin, was the minister of king Akbar. He was a very religious man and was in the habit of always saying, "whatever happens is for the best, it is God's will."

One morning, Akbar was getting a haircut and his fingernails trimmed. Accidentally one of his fingers was cut during the trimming.

Now some of the other ministers around the king were jealous of Birbal and the influence he had on the king. Knowing of Birbal's habit they ran to him to report the accident, hoping to get him into trouble with the king.

Predictably Birbal answered by saying, "Whatever happened is for the best, it is God's will." The ministers immediately ran back to the king to report what Birbal had said. Akbar became very upset. "How dare Birbal speak that way towards the king?" said Akbar. "Arrest him and throw him into the dungeon!," he ordered. The order was immediately carried out.

Now it so happened that the king went out hunting that day and during the heat of the hunt he was separated from the rest of the party. Soon the king found himself alone in the forest.

In that forest there also lived a primitive tribe who were out looking for a human sacrifice to offer to their deity. They soon came across the king and thought he would make a perfect offering, so they captured him and took him back to their village. They made all the preparations and were about to sacrifice him when the head priest noticed the cut on the kings finger. This was considered a bad sign, since any offering to the deity had to be unblemished. Due to the kings cut he was not considered eligible for the sacrifice and was released.

As the king made his way back to his palace he was thinking of poor Birbal lying in the dungeon. "How right Birbal was," thought the king to himself, "having my finger cut accidentally was indeed for the best since it has now saved my life."

When he reached the palace the king personally went to the dungeon to release Birbal. When he saw him he said, "Oh Birbal, please forgive me, you were absolutely right, whatever happens is for the best," and he narrated his close encounter with death.

But after finishing the tale a question arose in the kings mind and he asked his minister, "Birbal, I now see how it was for the best that my finger was cut, but, what is the good in your having been arrested and thrown in the dungeon?"

"Ahh" said Birbal, "If I were not in the dungeon I would have been with you when you were captured, and there are no blemishes on *my* body."

Whatever happens really is for the best, even if that is not obvious to us at the time. One should always look for the good in everything. Try and see the benefit of every situation and trust in God, always remaining detached.

Your Needs Are Less

Once Mullah Nasrudin came out of a mosque and there were different beggars standing outside it's gates. The Mullah, like all good people decided to give some alms but remembered the scriptures injunction to consider well what you give.

He went to the first beggar and questioned him, "Do you drink and smoke cigarettes?" The beggar answered that he did.

"I suppose you also like to go to bars and spend time with women?," continued Nasrudin. The beggar again answered in the affirmative.

Nasrudin gave him a gold coin and went to the second beggar.

He asked the second beggar the same questions. "Do you drink and smoke cigarettes?," asked Nasrudin. The beggar was a *sadhu* and said, "No, I don't drink or smoke."

"Do you go out with girls to bars?" "Absolutely not," answered the sadhu. "Don't you know that I'm a monk?"

Nasrudin handed him a copper coin and started to walk off. But the second beggar said, "What is this, what kind of justice is this? You gave a gold coin to that other man and he had all those bad habits, while I have no such bad habits and you gave me a copper coin."

Nasrudin said, "Brother, calm yourself, that man has many needs, while your needs are few."

I recall Baba telling this story once when a seeker complained to him that since he had started spending time in the ashram his parents stopped sending him money. They were apparently unhappy that he was spending all of his time meditating, remembering God and chanting his name. It appeared that parents supported worldly children but not spiritual seekers.

The Root Of All Troubles

Near a certain fishing village the fishermen were catching fish. Suddenly a kite swooped down and snatched one of the fishes. At the sight of the fish in its beak, about a dozen crows started chasing the kite, making a lot of noise with their cawing, while trying to steal the fish. Whichever direction the kite flew with the fish, the crows followed it. The kite flew towards the east and the crows followed it. The kite flew towards the west and still the crows followed it. The kite went north and south, but still the crows followed. They swooped down on him striking him in mid-air, not allowing him any peace to enjoy the fish.

The crows grew in number and as the kite became confused he started to fly in circles, and then he dropped the fish from its mouth. The crows at once let the kite alone and dove down after the fish, fighting among themselves. Relieved of its worries, the kite sat on the branch of a nearby tree and thought, "That wretched fish was at the root of all my troubles. Having gotten rid of it, I am now experiencing peace."

Desire is the fish, no sooner do we renounce it, we will enjoy peace.

That's Why You Are What You Are!

There was once a highly evolved and carefree soul. He wandered wherever he wished and was always in the habit of saying, "Yes, that's why you are what you are!"

One day he decided to visit the kings court. Outside the palace there were armed guards, and as they were ordinary people they barred his way. They were very rude to him and also gave him a few blows with their sticks.

He looked at them and simply said, "Yes, that's why you are what you are!"

He somehow made his way past them but soon came across some of the inner palace guards. "Where do you think you're going Babaji?," asked the officers.

The great being only said, "Yes, that is why you are what you are!," and kept going.

Meanwhile the prime minister noticed him and decided to follow him and see what would happen.

The great being next came across the head guards and the men asked politely, "Oh Maharaj, where are you going?"

Laughing, he answered, "Yes, that's why you are what you are!," and walked on.

He next met the highest ranking officer who greeted him with respect and asked, "Come Babaji, where are going, may I guide you?"

But the great being had only one mantra, "Yes, that's why you are what you are!"

He finally arrived at the kings court. When the king saw him, he got up from his throne, bowed to him and welcomed him with great respect and offered the saint a seat next to his.

"How are you Babaji, is everything well with you?," asked the king.

The great soul smiling, answered, "Yes, that's why you are what you are!"

Now the prime minister, who had been following him all this time, went up and bowed to him and asked, "Babaji, I have been watching you move throughout the palace and whenever anyone said anything to you, you always answered in the same way, `Yes, that's why you are what you are!' Please tell me what is the meaning of this statement?"

"That is how it is," answered the great soul. "A person is what he is because of *what* he is."

The prime minister said, "I don't understand the meaning of this, please explain what you mean."

The sadhu answered, "When I arrived at the front gate of the palace, the guards there stopped me with their sticks and even beat me. They are simple people without much intelligence, so they have to stand there all day. They also have no opportunity of seeing the inside of the court. So, you see, that is why they are what they are. Next I came across the inner palace guards. They are a bit more intelligent and therefore are trusted to do service inside the palace. Though they tried to stop me they did not beat me. Because of what they are, they are also paid better then those outside.

"Then, I met the head guards. They asked me where I was going in a polite way. They are more competent men and are also respected. They also receive a higher salary and it is so because of who they are.

"After that I met the most senior officer. He spoke to me with great respect and said I could enter the court. That is the quality of his understanding and compassion, so I said, `That's why you are what you are.'

"When I entered the court the king got up from his seat and welcomed me with great respect and inquired about my welfare, so he's the ruler, the master of the kingdom. That is why he is what he is, because of his own understanding. And you, Oh prime minister, were following me and listening quietly to everything, and finally asked me the meaning of my actions. You have the mind necessary to run the state, and that is why you are what you are!"

A person views himself and others according to the understanding of his own mind. We experience pleasure and pain according to the measure of our own intelligence.

God's Holy Name

O nce, the Nineteenth Century mystic Sri Ramakrishna, was given a talk on the power of God's name. He was saying, "Do not exhaust yourself by resorting to difficult practices. Just keep repeating the Name of God and you will realize Him in a very simple and natural manner."

Among the listeners was a well known surgeon who was also a cynic. He stood up and interrupted the master saying, "You've been going on and on about the wonders of the divine name, it doesn't make any sense to me. What's the point of saying a word over and over again? Can a man fill his stomach saying bread, bread, bread?"

Ramakrishna, who had never abused anyone in his life, suddenly shouted, "Shut up you bastard and sit down!"

On hearing this, the man completely lost his composure. His face got red with anger and his body began to tremble. He tried to speak but could not.

Ramakrishna put his hands together and pleaded with him saying, "Oh sir, calm down, calm down, what has happened to you?"

"You are asking me to be calm, after you have insulted me in front of everyone! How dare you?"

Ramakrishna asked, "But what have I done? Where is my fault?"

The man said, "You dare to feign ignorance, to pretend you don't know what has happened! You called me a bastard."

"Look," Ramakrishna said, "I called you a bastard just once, and look how it has affected you? You have lost your composure and your body started to shake violently. I only answered your question in the manner it was put. I used one word and it has changed you entirely. When an ordinary term of abuse can produce such an effect, what makes you think that God's Holy Name will have none?" The surgeon was at once silenced.

The Man With Forty Forms

There was once a magician who received a boon from a spirit. He was giving the power to duplicate himself into forty identical forms. The man went about committing different crimes but was never caught. Every time the authorities would come to arrest him, he would multiply himself into forty identical forms, and no one could tell the real man from the imitations.

He was extremely proud of his abilities and thought himself the most clever person alive.

Finally, his time of death arrived and he saw from a distance the messengers of Yama, the lord of death, coming to get him. As they got closer he multiplied himself into forty identical forms. When the messengers saw this, they became perplexed and did not know what to do. They could not figure out which one of the forms was the real man and so they left.

The man's ego became even larger, if that were possible. He now thought himself to be invincible. He thought to himself, "Even the messengers of death can not touch me, I'll live forever."

Meanwhile, the messengers had returned to Lord Yama and told him what had happened. They apologized to him for not being able to fulfill their task, but Lord Yama told them not to worry. He called one of his senior aides and told him to go and get the man, but before he left Yama whispered something in his ear.

The magician saw the messenger approaching and he again multiplied himself into forty forms.

As Yama's messenger arrived, he looked up and down at all the forms, they were absolutely identical. If a hand moved, the hand of all the others moved, if the eyes closed, all the eyes closed. If there was a turn to the right, all turned to the right. The messenger walked up and down, looking at the forms very carefully. As he walked, his head shook with astonishment and he was saying, "Fantastic, amazing, what perfection. I can not tell one from the other." He praised the man for his cleverness, saying, "These forms are absolutely perfect, there is no way to tell between one and another, but, he said, there is just one *tiny* flaw." Hearing the criticism, the man became incensed and he jumped out of the line and said, "What do you mean a flaw?" Immediately the messenger grabbed him and dragged him away.

Ego and pride are the root of all difficulties. When the balloon of ego over inflates, it will tend to burst.

The Correct Method Of Worship

Once, a poor simple peasant was praying to God saying, "Oh God, kindly come into my humble hut. I don't know the correct method of worshipping you since I have not studied the Koran, the Gita or the Bible. I have only love for you in my heart. Dear Lord, if you visit me I will make you comfortable. I will prepare a warm bath for you and serve you delicious food."

Meanwhile, Hazrat Musa, a religious teacher, happened to pass by and overheard the peasant's prayer. He stuck his head in the door of the hut and called out, "Hey, what are you talking about, come out here."

The poor man came out of his hut and saluted Hazrat Musa. Hazrat Musa asked, "What were you saying?"

The peasant said, "I was supplicating God, asking him to please visit my hut. I was telling him how I would take care of him and make him comfortable."

Hazrat Musa said, "You foolish sinner. Don't you know you have committed a gross heresy? God does not have a body, nor is he like a man that you can invite to your home. You have insulted God, and you have insulted religion."

The simple peasant became very frightened and said, "Oh, I have indeed made a mistake. I am very sorry. Please forgive me, I'll never do it again."

Hazrat Musa said, "Make sure you don't commit such sacrilege again," and went his way.

When he reached home, Hazrat Musa went into his prayer room and started praying, of course according to scriptural rules. In the middle of his prayers, he suddenly heard a voice from heaven saying, "Oh Musa, it was not that poor peasant who committed a sin, but you. You were sent into the world to bring more hearts to me, not to confuse people with differences of high and low. Yet tonight you turned a man away who's heart was already open to me."

Go Forward!

Once upon a time a wood cutter went into a forest to chop wood. There he met a sadhu. The holy man said to him, "My friend, go forward!" On returning home the wood cutter asked himself, "Why did that sadhu tell me to go forward?"

Some time passed and one day he remembered the sadhu's words. He said to himself, "Today I'll go deeper into the forest."

Going deeper into the forest he discovered innumerable sandal-wood trees. He was very happy and returned with a cart load of sandal-wood trees. Selling them in the market he became very rich.

A few days later he again remembered the words of the sadhu to go forward. He decided to go deeper into the forest and discovered a silver-mine near a river. This was beyond his expectation. He dug out the silver from the mine and sold it in the market. He made a great deal of money.

A few days more passed. One day he thought, "The holy man didn't ask me to stop at the silver-mine, he told me to go forward." This time he went to the other side of the river and found a gold-mine. The man exclaimed, "Ahh! This is why the sadhu asked me to go forward!"

After a few more days he went deeper into the forest and found a diamond mine. He now became extremely rich.

Whatever you do, you will find better and better things if you only continue going forward. In the spiritual life one may feel a little intoxication as a result of a little practice. But we should not conclude from this that we have achieved everything that there is to achieve. The more you advance, the more you will see that there are other things even beyond the sandalwood forest, mines of silver, gold, and even precious gems. Always go forward!

Svetaketu

When Svetaketu was twelve years old his father Uddalaka Aruni said to him, "Svetaketu, you should now go to a Guru and receive your education. All of our ancestors have been properly educated in the Vedas and were knowers of Brahman."

The young boy obeyed his father and went to a teacher where he studied for twelve years. After memorizing all the Vedas, he returned home full of pride in his learning. When his father saw him, he could at once perceive that his son had become a man of learning, but that he had not achieved any spiritual knowledge. His father asked him, "Svetaketu, have you asked for that knowledge by which knowing, all else is known, by which we hear the unhearable, by which we perceive the unperceivable?"

Svetaketu asked, "Dear father, what is that knowledge? I have not heard of that wondrous knowledge. Please teach it to me."

"My child," answered his father, "it is like this. When you understand the essential nature of a lump of clay, you then know all things made of clay, the difference being only in name and form, but the truth is that all are clay; when you know the essential nature of gold, all things made of gold are then known, the difference being only in name and form, but in truth, all is gold - so is that knowledge, knowing which we know all. Therefore, know the essence of things, that which underlies this vast and diverse mass of names and forms.

"In the beginning," continued the father, "there was pure Being, one without a second. Some say that in the beginning there was non-existence, and that out of that the universe was born. But how could such a thing be? How could existence be born of non-existence? No, my son, in the beginning there was Existence alone - One only, without a second. He, the One, thought to himself, 'Let me be many, let me grow forth.' In this way he projected the universe out of himself, and, having projected out of himself the universe, he entered into every being and every thing. All that is has its self in Him alone. He is the truth. He is the subtle essence of all. He is the Self of all. And That, Svetaketu, That Art Thou."

After listening to all this, Svetaketu said, "Please tell me more about this Self," and then asked, "Father, where does a man go when he sleeps?"

The father continued, "As bees make honey by gathering juices from many flowering plants and trees, and as these juices are reduced to one honey and do not know from what flowers its parts have come from, similarly my son, all creatures, when they are merged in that one Existence, whether in deep sleep or in death, know nothing of their past or present state. Because of the ignorance covering them, they know not that they are merged in him and that from him they come.

"Whatever these creatures are, whether a tiger, or a lion, or a worm, or a gnat, or a mosquito, that they remain after they come back from the state of deep sleep.

"All these have their self in Him alone. He is the truth. He is the subtle essence of all. He is the Self. And That, Svetaketu, That Art Thou."

Svetaketu asked, "Dear father, but why can I not see this Self in this body?"

His father answered, "Svetaketu, put some salt crystals into a bowl of water before going to sleep tonight, and come to me tomorrow morning."

The obedient son did as he was told. The next morning his father asked him to bring the salt crystals which he had put into the bowl of water.

Svetaketu was puzzled and asked, "Father, how is it possible to remove the salt from the water?"

Then Uddalaka said, "All right. Can you see the salt?"

Svetaketu said, "No, I can not see it."

"Then just taste the water," said the father. "How does it taste?"

The boy tasted the water and said, "Why, it tastes salty of course."

"My dear child," said the father, "in the same way, though you do not see Brahman in this body, he is indeed here. That which is the subtle essence, in that have all things their existence. That is the truth. That is the Self. And That, Svetaketu, That Art Thou."

This dialogue between Uddalaka and his son Svetaketu is narrated in the Chandogya Upanishad.

Nasrudin and the Miser

One day, Nasrudin's wife was criticizing him for being poor. "If you are a man of religion," she said, "you should pray for money. If that is your profession, you should be paid for it, just as anyone else is paid."

"Very well," said Nasrudin, "I shall do just that."

Going into the garden, the Mullah shouted at the top of his voice, "Oh God! I have served you all these years without financial gain. My wife now says that I should be paid. May I therefore, and at once, have a hundred gold pieces of my outstanding salary?"

A miser who lived next door just happened to be on his roof counting his riches when he heard the Mullahs prayer. Thinking that he would make a fool of Nasrudin, he threw down in front of him a bag containing exactly a hundred gold coins.

"Thank you Lord!," shouted Nasrudin, and hurried into the house.

He showed the coins to his wife, who was very impressed. "Forgive me," she said, "I never really believed that you were a saint, but I now see that you are."

During the next few days, the miser noticed many luxuries items being delivered to the Mullah's house. He started becoming anxious and presented himself at Nasrudin's door.

The Mullah said, "Know Oh friend that I am a saint. What can I do for you?"

"I want my money back," said the miser. "I was the one who threw down the bag of gold coins, not God."

"You may have been the instrument, but the gold did not come as a result of my asking you for it," answered Nasrudin.

The miser became very agitated and said, "I'll take you to court, and I will have justice."

Nasrudin agreed and they started off to the Magistrate. As soon as they were outside the house Nasrudin said to the miser, "I am dressed in rags. If I appear beside you before the magistrate, the difference in our appearances may prejudice the court in your favor."

"Very well," snarled the miser, "take my robe."

They had gone just a few yards further when Nasrudin said, "You are riding on a horse and I am on foot. If we appear like this before the judge he may think that he should give the verdict to you."

"I know who is going to win this case," shouted the miser, "no matter what he looks like! But you can ride on my horse if you wish."

Nasrudin mounted the horse, and his neighbor walked behind him. When their turn came, the miser explained to the judge what had happened.

"And what do you have to say to this charge?" the judge asked the Mullah.

"Your honor," started Nasrudin, "this man is a miser, and he is also suffering from delusions. He has the illusion that he gave me the money. But in reality, it came from a higher source. It merely appeared to this man to have been given by him."

"But can you prove that?" asked the judge.

"There is nothing simpler," answered Nasrudin. "His obsessions take the form of thinking that things belong to him when they do not. Just ask him to whom this robe belongs?"

"That is mine!" shouted the Miser.

"Now," said Nasrudin, "ask him whose horse I was riding when I came to this court."

"You were riding my horse!" screamed the miser.

"Case dismissed," declared the judge.

Don't Brood Over The Sins Of Others

An ascetic used to live by the side of a temple. Right across the road from him lived a prostitute. Seeing the constant flow of men going into the prostitute's house, the monk one day called her and abused her saying, "You are a great sinner. You sin day and night. Oh, how miserable will be your reward hereafter."

The poor prostitute became extremely sorry for her misdeeds, and with a genuine repentance she prayed to God asking His forgiveness. But since prostitution had been her only profession, she could not easily adopt any other means of earning her livelihood. And so, whenever her flesh sinned, she always reproached herself and prayed to God more and more for forgiveness.

Meanwhile, the ascetic saw that his advice had apparently produced no effect upon her, and thought, "Let me see how many men visits this woman in the course of her life." And from that day onwards, whenever a man entered her house, the ascetic counted them by putting a pebble aside, and in course of time there arose a big heap of pebbles.

One day the acetic said to the prostitute, pointing to the heap, "Woman, do you see this heap? Each pebble stands for your indulgence in sin since I first advised you of your evil course. Beware of your evil deeds!"

The poor woman began to tremble at the sight of the accumulation of her sins, and she prayed to God shedding tears of utter helplessness, inwardly repeating, "Lord, will you not free me from this miserable life which I am leading?" Her prayer was heard, since on that very day she died.

By the strange will of God, the ascetic also died on the same day. Gods messengers came down from Heaven and carried the spirit of the prostitute to the heavenly regions, while the messengers of Death bound the spirit of the ascetic and carried him down to the nether world.

The ascetic, seeing the good fortune of the prostitute cried out loud, "Is this the subtle justice of God? I spent all my life in poverty and the practice of asceticism, and I'm being carried to hell, while that prostitute, whose life was always spent in sin, is going to Heaven!"

Hearing this, the messengers of God said, "The decrees of God are always just; as you think, so shall you reap. You passed your life in external show and vanity, trying to get honor and fame; and God has given you this. Your heart never sincerely yearned after him. This prostitute earnestly prayed to God day and night, though her body sinned all the time. Look at the treatment which your body and her body are receiving from those below. As you never sinned with your body, they have decorated it with flowers and garlands, and are carrying it with music in procession to the sacred river. But this prostitute's body, which had sinned, is being torn to pieces at this very moment by vultures and jackals. Nevertheless, she was pure in heart and is therefore going to the realm of the pure. Your heart was always absorbed in contemplating her sins and therefore became impure. You are therefore going to the realm of the impure."

The Master's Shoes

The saint Nizamuddin was well known throughout the Muslim world, and it is said that no one who ever approached him went away empty handed. Once, a poor farmer went to meet him to ask for help. The farmer had three daughters that were at the marriageable age but he had no money to perform their weddings. He asked the saint for help, knowing that many wealthy devotees used to visit him.

The saint said, "All right, sit here with me and whatever comes in the way of offerings you may take with you." The poor man sat there all day but for some unknown reason not a single coin came. The second and third day also brought nothing. Nizamuddin said to the farmer, "This is quite strange, usually something comes. I don't know what to tell you, but here, take these old pair of shoes of mine and perhaps someone will offer you something for them."

The poor man accepted them and left for his village. Along the way he stopped to rest underneath a tree. He was very disappointed and was thinking what could he get for an old pair of shoes. He even thought of throwing them away.

But it so happened that a merchant was passing by on his way to Delhi. He had nine camels with him loaded with goods like silk cloth, grains, gold and silver. He noticed the man sitting underneath the tree looking dejected and asked him what was the matter.

The poor farmer recounted to him how he had gone to the saint Nizamuddin in order to get some money for his daughters weddings. But even after sitting with him for three days he still had not received any donations and so the saint had offered him this old pair of shoes, and told him to try and get something for them.

When the merchant Amir Khusro, for that was who it was, heard this and realized that the old pair of shoes belonged to his Guru Nizamuddin, he made an offer for them to the farmer. "I'll give you eight of my camels, loaded with all their goods for those shoes," he said. The poor man was ecstatic and eagerly agreed.

Amir Khusro took the old shoes, placing them in a silk scarf, and continued towards Delhi. When he reached Delhi he went to visit Nizamuddin. He prostrated himself at the saints feet and then sat down.

Nizamuddin noticed the bundle that Amir Khusro was clutching close to him and asked what it was. Amir Khusro showed him his old shoes and explained how he acquired them.

Nizamuddin asked, "My son, how much did you pay for such an old pair of shoes?"

Amir Khusro answered humbly, that he had given the farmer eight camels loaded with goods of cloth, grain, gold and silver.

Nizamuddin smiled and replied, "Ahh, you got them dirt cheap!"

This was one of my Guru's favorite stories. Being extremely devoted to his own Guru, he had realized the true value of the masters blessings.

Begging From A Beggar

O nce, when King Akbar was riding his horse in the countryside surrounding the city of Agra, he became hungry and asked a peasant for some food. The peasant, who thought he was an ordinary traveler, gave him some food and water and made him comfortable.

When Akbar was ready to leave he told the peasant, "My good man, I am the king of India. If you ever are in need of anything, please come to me without hesitation. I will be glad to help you."

After some months the peasant did have some needs and thought the king might be able to help him. He therefore went to Agra and asked to see the king.

He was soon ushered into the King's private chamber, where at the moment Akbar was engaged in prayer. At the end of his prayers the King with raised hands began asking for a number of gifts from God.

When the King rose from his knees and saw the peasant, he greeted the man warmly and asked if there was something he could do for him.

The peasant humbly asked the King what he was doing and the King replied that he was asking God for wealth for his kingdom, and to help him in solving the many difficulties that he faced.

"Thank you Sir," said the peasant, "May I now have your per-mission to leave?"

"But you have not asked for anything!," exclaimed the king. "Did you not come here for some help?"

The peasant answered, "Sire, I will beg at the same door as the one you are begging from. For my Lord, though you are the greatest of kings, I find that you are also a poor beggar. And for me to beg of a beggar would be a disgrace."

Yajnavalkya and Maitreyi

The great sage Yajnavalkya had two wives named Maitreyi and Katyayani. Of the two, Maitreyi was a real seeker, while Katyayani was, like all other ordinary women, attached to worldly objects.

After leading a householders life for many years, the rishi Yajnavalkya decided to renounce the world and live like a sannyasin. He therefore called Maitreyi and Katyayani and said to them, "I am thinking of renouncing the world and therefore wish to divide my property between you two before I go."

Katyayani accepted her share of Yajnavalkya's possessions but the spiritually minded Maitreyi said, "Dear one, you are talking of dividing your property between us, but tell me, if this whole earth belonged to me, with all its wealth, will I attain immortality, will I know the Self?"

Yajnavalkya replied, "No my dear, not at all. Your life would be very comfortable like the rich but no one could hope to obtain immortality through wealth."

Maitreyi then said, "Then what do I need wealth for? Instead, please tell me the way to that spiritual knowledge, for that is what I truly desire."

Yajnavalkya was elated at hearing Maitreyi's request. He took her aside and said lovingly, "You have always been dear to me Maitreyi, and now you ask to know about that truth which is nearest my heart. I shall teach you and so listen attentively and meditate constantly on what I shall tell you."

He continued, "It is not for the sake of the husband, my beloved, that the husband is dear, but for the sake of the Self.

"It is not for the sake of the wife, that the wife is dear, but for the sake of the Self.

"It is not for the sake of the children, that the children are dear, but for the sake of the Self.

"It is not for the sake of itself, my dear, that anything whatsoever is esteemed, but for the sake of the Self.

"It is for the sake of the inner Self that man loves all other things. That is the uppermost motive of our love for things.

"That Spirit, Oh Maitreyi, that inner Self, is the one thing that really deserves to be seen, to be heard of, to be thought about, and meditated upon. The knowledge of that Self makes everything else known. Where there is consciousness of the Self, individuality is no more."

Maitreyi was not clear on this point and she asked, "You say `Where there is consciousness of the Self, individuality is no more', this statement confuses me, please elaborate."

Yajnavalkya said, "My dear, don't be confused by what I have said. But meditate deeply on the truth I have spoken. As long as there is duality, one sees the other, one hears the other, one smells the other, one speaks to the other, one thinks of the other, one knows the other; but when for the illumined soul the all is dissolved in the Self, who is there to be seen, and by whom; who is there to be heard, and by whom; who is there to be spoken to, and by whom; who is there to be known, and by whom? My dear Maitreyi, the Intelligence which reveals all - by what shall it be revealed? By whom shall the Knower be known? The Self is described as not This, not That. It is incomprehensible, for it cannot be comprehended; undecaying, for it never decays; unattached, for it never attaches itself. By whom, Oh my beloved, shall the Knower be known? This is the truth of immortality. This, Oh

Maitreyi, is that highest knowledge. Meditate on That, realize That"

This dialogue between Yajnavalkya and his wife Maitreyi is recorded in the Brihadaranyaka Upanishad.

The Middle Way

The Buddha had been reduced to a mere skeleton by many years of fasts. But with all this he still did not feel like he was getting closer to his goal. He thought very deeply about what to do, but he could come to no conclusions. One day, as he sat meditating quietly near a river banks, he overheard a conversation between two musicians. One was saying to the other, "You should not make the strings too tight, otherwise they may break, nor should they be too loose, since then the sound will not be correct. They should in fact not be too tight, nor too loose."

When the Buddha heard these words, they had a deep effect on him. He concluded that a middle path was needed. He had become very weak from the many fasts and realized that good health was needed for spiritual progress.

The Waterless Well

Once a man wanted to dig a well and someone advised him to dig in a certain spot, so he did. But after digging down about 20 feet and still finding no water, he became disheartened.

In the meantime another man came along, and laughing at his foolish attempt advised him to dig in another spot, which in his opinion he said was the best place to dig for water. So the man went and started to dig at the new spot. This time he dug down 25 feet, but still found no water.

A third man came and asked him to try in another, and better place, which he would point out to him. He started digging at the new location and went down 30 feet, but although it was deeper there still was no water.

Completely exhausted he became disgusted and was about to give up the task, when a fourth man came along and said, "My dear fellow, you have been working very hard, but at the wrong spot. Let me show you the perfect spot for a well. You will find water there in no time at all."

The man started digging again and he went down 35 feet but there was still no water. The poor man became absolutely disgusted and exhausted and gave up the task altogether.

If the man had the patience and perseverance to dig half of the total number of feet in only one spot, he would have certainly found water. Often seekers go from one teacher to another, one technique to another. The person may have some experiences but real transformation never occurs. One should be one pointed, only then will something be achieved. One should find a real Guru and perform intense spiritual practices under his care. After all, what can't a man attain if he takes the necessary trouble?

Arjuna, What Do You See?

Once Dronacharya, the great martial arts teacher of the young Pandava princes, decided to test the comparative abilities of his pupils. After completing their education in the use of arms he assembled them together. He had put an artificial bird, which was to be the target, on top of a neighboring tree. When they were all together, Drona said, "Take up your bows and arrows and stand ready to hit and cut off the head of that bird when I give the order. I'll give each of you a turn, one by one."

Dronacharya first called the eldest Pandava, Yudhishthira, saying, "Aim your arrow and be ready to shoot when I command you."

Yudhishthira aimed at the bird, waiting for the order to fire. But Dronacharya said, "Look at the bird on top of the tree."

"I see it," said Yudhishthira.

"Do you see me, your brothers and the tree?"

Yudhishthira answered, "I see you, my brothers, the tree and the bird."

Dronacharya asked the question a number of times, but Yudhishthira gave the same answer each time. Drona then said, "Stand aside Yudhishthira, you are not ready to hit the mark."

Dronacharya then called Bhima and said, "Get set and aim at the target Bhima, and fire when I give the command."

Bhima stood ready, taking aim at the bird. Then Drona asked

him the same questions he had put to Yudhishthira. "What do you see Bhima, do you see me, your brothers, the tree and the bird?"

Bhima gave the same reply, "I see you, my brothers, the tree and the bird."

Instead of given the command to fire, Drona said, "Step aside Bhima, you are not ready to hit the target."

Dronacharya then called on Duryodhana and then the twins Nakula and Sahadeva. He put the same questions to them one after the other and they all gave the same answer. "We see you, the other princes, the tree and the bird." Drona also asked them to stand aside.

Finally he called Arjuna. Drona said, "Arjuna take your aim at the bird and fire when I give the command." Drona then put the same questions to him saying, "Arjuna, what do you see, do you see me, your brothers, the tree and the bird?"

"I see only the bird," answered Arjuna, "not you, not the others, nor the tree."

Dronacharya then said, "If you see the bird, then describe it to me."

Arjuna said, "I see only the head of the bird, not its body."

Ecstatic on hearing Arjuna's answer, Dronacharya shouted, "Then shoot!" Arjuna fired the arrow ~ and struck the birds head, severing it from its body.

Due to his great concentration and dexterity, Arjuna became known as the greatest archer of his time.

The Royal Guru

Amritrai was a perfected being and a royal Guru, he was known as the Guru of kings. He used to always sit on a silver throne, wearing regal robes embroidered with gold. He was always surrounded by wealth.

Amritrai was also a poet and composed a number of songs, and he used to hold daily religious programs as well. One day he was singing one of his songs which went like this, "These possessions are but dust, and no intelligent person will seek them, for they are ephemeral and have absolutely no value. Who will go after fleeting possessions, and why should anyone build these enormous palaces? A humble hut is much better. What need has anyone for majestic royal robes? Isn't it much better to find patches of cloth and sew them into a quilt to cover your body? I feel like going from house to house begging alms for food."

One man in the audience was quite learned, and he exclaimed, "What on earth are you talking about?"

Amritrai said, "What I am saying is absolutely true."

The man snapped back, "It's all right for you to talk like that! You sit on a silver throne, you wear royal robes, and you eat from golden plates; so you can easily scorn possessions."

Amritrai replied, "Oh learned sir, what shall I do? These things are due to my *karma*. It torments me and will not leave me alone!"

"Is that so?," challenged the man. "All right, come with me tomorrow; we will go for a walk in the forest."

The next day, Amritrai and the scholar found their way to a se-

98

cluded corner of the forest where they discovered a straw hut. The scholar said, "I am going to beg for food. Wait for me here until I return."

Now it so happened that on the other side of that same forest there lived a great king who happened to be out on a hunt that day. As they were preparing for lunch, the king commanded some of his soldiers to go and search for an ascetic to share their meal, as was the custom. The soldiers set out on their horses looking in the forest for a holy man. After riding for some time they came across Amritrai, who was sitting quietly under a tree next to the hut. The soldiers took him back to the king. The king immediately recognized him as the royal Guru, Amritrai. The king was very happy at his good fortune and placed the Guru on his own throne and fed him from his own golden plates.

Meanwhile, the scholar, returning from his begging, happened to pass by the kings camp and noticed the Guru sitting on a royal seat, and eating in his usual regal manner. The scholar was amazed.

When Amritrai spotted the scholar, he shouted, "Oh learned sir, see how my karma torments me! Please deliver me from it!"

A Siddha, or a perfected being, is very pure. Even in the midst of wealth they are not effected by the wealth, and live simple lives.

The Cobbler's Gift

Once King Pipa, a wealthy *Rajput* monarch, had heard of the cobbler saint Ravi Das. Having a desire for spiritual upliftment he wanted to meet the saint, but at the same time he felt embarrassed to be seen visiting a lower caste person.

But one day a fair was being held outside the capital and all the people left their homes to visit the fair. The Raja thought this was a good opportunity to visit the great saint without being seen.

The king reached the saints hut where he found him soaking leather in a bucket of water.

Not wanting to waste time, the king said, "Holy Sir, will you please initiate me?"

Ravi Das, taking a cup of water from the bucket said, "Oh king, have some of this water as a gift from me."

Not having sufficient faith, the king was repulsed by the idea. He decided to deceive the saint by pretending to drink the water. He was wearing a long sleeve shirt which was tightly fastened at the wrists. So, instead of drinking the leather-water, he poured it slowly down the sleeves of his shirt. Ravi Das was of course aware of this but he remained silent.

After the king had finished pretending to drink the water, the saint said, "That is enough for now. You may now go, I will complete the initiation later."

The king bowed and stepping outside of the hut, he looked in both directions making sure he was not seen by anyone. Since everyone was still at the fair no one saw him.

When he reached the palace he sent for his washerman and asked him to clean the shirt. The washerman noticed the stains in the shirt and asked the king what had happened. The king told him about his visit to the cobbler Ravi Das and explained to him how the shirt got stained. The washerman took the shirt home but because he was busy, he asked his daughter to clean it, telling her how the king had stained the shirt.

The young girl had heard the greatness of Ravi Das so she started to chew the stained parts of the shirt in order to remove the stains, but instead of spitting out the leather-water, she swallowed it. As she did this she was transformed. She went into a deep meditation and started experiencing her own inner Self. In a short time her whole life was completely changed. Soon the whole neighborhood came to know that she had been transformed from a simple girl into a great saint.

As word spread throughout the city, the story also reached the king. Being still unhappy, the king decided to visit the young girl.

Seeing the king, the girl bowed to him. But the king said, "My child, I have not come to you as a ruler but to beg from you spiritual enlightenment."

The young girl replied, "Your majesty, whatever I have received is due to your grace."

The king was surprised at her reply, and asked her what she meant.

"Oh Raja," she said, "the secret of my transformation was in your shirt. Having sucked the water stains from it, the inner spiritual power was awakened."

Immediately realizing his stupidity, the king remembered his meeting with the great saint Ravi Das. Giving up his arrogance the king ran to the cobblers hut. This time with true humility bowed to the saint and asked for his blessing.

Ravi Das said, "Oh king, when you first visited me, I thought here is a great king coming to the humble hut of a poor cobbler. I therefore wished to give you something which you would remember with pleasure throughout your life. You thought the water which I offered you was the water I had been soaking my leather in, but in fact it was true nectar. Do to your misfortune, it was the washerman's daughter who received the gift. But don't fear, I will initiate you with a sacred *mantra*, and repeating it with devotion you will gain everything."

The Saint's Begging-Bowl

Once, a *dervish* stopped a king who was riding his horse through the streets. The king became angry and said, "How dare you, a man of no value, interrupt the advancement of your sovereign?"

The dervish, holding out his begging-bowl answered, "Can you be a king if you cannot even fill my begging-bowl?"

The King ordered his attendant to fill the dervishes bowl with gold coins. But as soon as the bowl appeared to be full of coins, then they disappeared, and the bowl seemed empty again.

Bag after bag of gold was brought, and still the bowl appeared to devour the coins.

"Stop!" shouted the King, "for this rascal is emptying my treasury!"

"To you I am emptying your treasury," said the Dervish, "but to others I am merely illustrating a truth."

"And what is that truth?" asked the King.

"The truth is, that the bowl is the desire of man, and the gold what man is given. There is no end to man's capacity to devour, without being in any way changed. You see, the bowl has eaten nearly all your wealth, but it is still just a gourd, and has not partaken of the nature of gold in any way."

"If you care," continued the Dervish, "step into the bowl, it will devour you too. How then, can a king consider himself of any importance?"

I Am Everything!

There was once a great saint named Hazrat Basjid Bastami, who was a great devotee of God. One day, during his meditation he completely lost consciousness of individuality, and filled with ecstasy he cried out, "I am God, I am the light of the world, I am everything."

When his disciples who were sitting outside his room heard this, they were astonished. When Hazrat Bastami came out of his room the disciples asked, "Oh revered Hazrat, what did you mean when you shouted, `I am God, I am everything'. This goes against the teachings of Islam. You have committed a great sin."

Bastami simply answered, "I don't believe I said that, it must have been someone else. But if I should say such a thing in the future, then punish me according to the Islamic law."

Just a few days later while meditating, Hazrat Bastami again started shouting, "I am God, I am everything, I am God."

As soon as the disciples heard this, they rushed to grab whatever weapons they could find and started to attack Hazrat. Some struck him on the head, while others kicked him on his sides, arms and legs. But then a most amazing thing happened. The disciples found that every blow they inflicted on Bastami the resulting pain was experienced by them. The more they struck him, the more pain they themselves experienced. Meanwhile Bastami continued to shout, "I am God, I am the light of the world, I am everything."

In order to save themselves, they had to stop beating him. After sometime he came out of his deep meditation, and noticing his disciples bruised and in pain asked, "What has happened to you?"

The disciples said, "We struck you, but we ourselves experienced the results."

"Why did you strike me?" asked Bastami.

"Because you were shouting, "I am God, I am everything, all this is me, I am the Spirit within everyone."

"That is the reason why you received the fruits of your own blows," said Hazrat, "because what I was shouting is true, I am each one of you. If that were not so, you would not have experienced the results of your own aggression."

Nasrudin's Vow

Once, Nasrudin was completely broke, he had no money at all. He was walking along the highway and he prayed to God saying, "Oh God, please help me, let me find some money. If you grant me this prayer I vow to use part of it for a special offering to you at the mosque."

After walking for sometime all of a sudden he noticed an old coin on the ground. Nasrudin became very excited, but as he continued to walk he started to rethink about his vow to God. He started thinking, "Perhaps I was to hasty in making that vow, I should have waited just a little longer."

He finally reached a small town and took the coin to the money changer. When the money changer saw that it was an old and worn out coin he did not give Nasrudin the full value but only 75% of the value of a new coin. Nasrudin was very disappointed. As he was leaving the shop he said, "Ahh, how clever you are Oh Lord, seeing that you have already taken your portion."

We often think that we are very clever. Many people's minds work like this. Sometimes a resolve is made to follow a certain teaching, but due to an impure mind, it may unconsciously perform such tricks. Baba used to say that God is concealed due to man's cleverness of mind. When self-deception is removed God is revealed. We are betrayed by our wrong understanding. We should not forget our promises to God.

The Most Useless Thing

Once a seeker went to a saint and, with a great show of humility said, "Master, I am a very low person. Tell me how I am to be saved." Now the seeker was an advanced *Hatha Yogi* and was very proud of his physical accomplishments.

The saint, reading the heart of the man told him, "I will teach you, but first you must bring me the Guru's *dakshina*." Now it is customary to bring a gift when one approaches the Guru for instructions. The seeker said, "Yes of course, I will bring anything that you like." The Guru said, "Go and bring me the most filthy and useless thing, that which nobody wants."

The seeker went away in search of the sort of thing the Guru had asked for. He looked everywhere; in caves, on mountains, and in forests, but could not find anything that would conform to the Guru's description - something that was not wanted or that couldn't be used by anybody. It seemed that everything he found was considered useful by somebody. He started thinking that perhaps there wasn't anything so useless.

But, the next morning, as he was relieving himself, the idea struck him that his feces could not be of any use to anyone. He started thinking, "There certainly isn't anything more filthy or more impure then this lump of shit. If I take this to the Guru, he will be pleased."

So he started to pick it up, when all of a sudden he heard a voice coming from it saying, "You wretched, filthy, dirty fellow. What are you doing? Don't touch me."

The seeker was taken aback. He was very proud of himself, belonging as he did to a high caste. He had been a celibate all his life, and he had lived a very pure life following all the scriptural injunctions. And yet here was some nasty creature in that filthy pile of shit who dared to call him low, who dared to insult him.

The seeker, addressing the creature in the shit said, "Why do you, who are foul-smelling and have flies hovering all around you call me low?"

The voice answered, "Do you know who I am? Before I began keeping company with you, I was very attractive and beautiful. I was fragrant wheat. I was pure vegetables and sweet fruits. I was delicious cake and ice cream. But keeping your company for just a few hours this is what happened to me. This is the wretched condition I have been reduced to. And yet you dare to touch me?"

Immediately realizing his arrogance the seeker understood the lesson and became humble. He returned to the Guru and offered his own body as the most useless thing.

The seeker learnt true humility. As a result he attained the highest perfection.

The Lion and the Sheep

Once a lioness was about to attack a herd of sheep. She was not well and had not eaten for many days. She was also about to give birth and was therefore very weak. Moving slowly in a crouching position she came to the edge of a meadow, eyeing the sheep with great concentration.

The sheep had not as yet noticed her and they continued grazing in perfect contentment. The lioness stood still, with eyes focused wide, she prepared to leap. Gathering all her strength she shot forward charging the group of sheep, but then suddenly she fell forward. She lay there breathing very hard, as if gasping for air. She had started to give birth. As she struggled for some time the sheep watched quietly from a distance. Soon, a lion cub was visible, but the lioness lay there motionless. Giving birth had taken everything out of her and she laid there dead.

After sometime one of the ewe's, who had herself recently given birth, noticed the baby cub, with eyes closed trying to crawl around in search of nourishment. Her motherly instincts immediately took over and she went over and laid down near the cub and started nursing him. Shortly, the other sheep came closer in order to have a better look. They noticed the dead lion and were all glad they had escaped her clutches. They also noticed the ewe next to it, nursing what they thought was her lamb. Soon they all went back to their grazing as if nothing had happened.

Days passed and soon months, the lion cub grew up among the other lambs. His playmates considered him a bit rough and others thought him peculiar. Even though they did not directly perceive him as not one of them, they sensed that he was somehow different. The lion cub himself did not know that he was not a sheep, but as he got older he too started to sense that he was different. Questions that he put to his mother gave him no satisfactory answers and she just encouraged him to try and blend in with the others.

As time passed he became more settled and appeared as normal as the rest of the sheep. He had also started hanging out with the Rams and this brought him some satisfaction.

In this way many months passed with the lion cub going about bleating and grazing like the other sheep. Then one night, he heard some twigs snap in the forest near the meadow. He turned his head towards the sound and noticed a dark figure sitting in the moonlight. His body was slender, his head large with a thick mane, and eyes bright as diamonds. He looked serene and self-assured. He was a majestic creature and the lion cub was quite impressed with the sight. But he soon thought that this must be a lion, a creature that his mother and the others had always warned him about. He started to feel some fear and was about to turn and run. But before he knew it, the lion had gone, disappearing into the forest night.

That night the young lion could hardly sleep. He could not erase that majestic figure from his mind. The next day he hoped that the lion would return, but he did not. Finally, after a few days the lion reappeared. In his excitement the young lion shouted, "The lion has returned!"

Hearing the cry the sheep scattered hear and there bleating in panic. But the young lion stood his ground. He was afraid, but at the same time excited at seeing the old lion again. He was certain the lion would pounce on him any moment and his body tensed up.

Then suddenly, he heard a low, deep roar coming from the lion, and the old lion said, "What is the matter, why are you afraid?"

The young lion answered, "I do not know. I am a sheep and have always been told that lions are our enemies."

"A sheep?" asked the old lion in surprise. "You are not a sheep, you are a lion just like me."

"No," said the young lion, "I am a sheep."

"You are a lion!" roared the old lion.

The young lion answered, "Yes, sir," but this response was out of fear rather then a belief in his true identity.

The old lion perceiving this, looked at him with compassion and shook his mane in disbelief. "Very well," he said, "let it be for now." "But if you wish, you may come to visit me in the forest, and we will talk some more."

The young lion said, "Yes, I would like that very much."

The old lion smiled and said, "Very well, come whenever you like," and he turned and left.

That night the young lion could not stop thinking of the old lion. He could not understand the old lion's statement. How could he be a lion, he thought to himself. Such doubts troubled him throughout the night.

The next morning, as the Sun rose, the young lion started for the forest. He had never before left the meadow and so this was a new adventure for him. As he got further into the forest he realized that he did not even know where the old lion lived. He started feeling anxious but he continued deeper into the forest. His anxiety turned into fear, and he thought, "What could a lion want with a sheep, except to eat it." He started thinking that perhaps this was a foolish move, that he should have stayed in the meadows with the other sheep, where he belonged.

But his desire to see the old lion again over-powered his fear and he moved on. Suddenly, the old lion was standing right in front of him. The young lion's fear left him and he was full of joy at the reunion.

The old lion said, "So, you have come. Very good. Will you stay with me?"

The young lion said, "Well, I had hoped to stay for a little while, but I should return to the meadow. The other sheep will worry about me."

"Why are you so concerned about the sheep, you are a lion, wake up."

The young lion remained silent.

The old lion said, "Come with me," and he took him to a nearby pool of clear water. "Look at your reflection in the water, and now look at me," he said. "What do you see? Aren't the images the same?" asked the old lion.

"Well, they do appear similar," answered the young lion.

"They are the same," roared the old lion. "You are a lion just like me."

"But how can I be a lion when I'm a sheep?" asked the young lion.

"You are not a sheep," the old lion said calmly, "I have been telling you that you are a lion."

"But..." the young lion started.

"There are no 'buts'," the old lion roared. "Now let me hear you roar," commanded the lion.

The young lion tried but all he could get out was a pathetic bleating.

"No, no," said the old lion, "like this," and he let out a loud roar.

"Can I really be a lion?" asked the young lion.

"Not only can you be a lion, but you already are a lion," answered the old lion. "You are not a sheep, you have always been a lion, but you have thought and acted like a sheep. Now, meditate on your own true nature and repeat, `I am a lion. I am a lion. Practice this everyday, and continue to look at your reflection in the pool."

The young lion remained in the forest and continued to practice the meditation the old lion taught him. His mind would often wander and he would recall the memories of his past association with the sheep. But gradually his mind became more focused and memories of his past eventually disappeared, until one full moon night, as he was repeating, "I am a lion, I am a lion," he started experiencing a tremendous power flowing through his body. He soon became conscious of his thick mane and strong body. At that moment he knew without a doubt that he was indeed a lion, and suddenly he let out a deep spontaneous roar.

The Flower Which Caused Pain

Mansur was in the habit of saying, "Ana~el~Haqq!, Ana~el~Haqq! (I am the Truth, I am God), that is, claiming that he was at one with the Lord. He was rebuked for this and was told to say instead, "He is the Truth."

Mansur replied, "Yes, He is all, but you say He is lost. Mansur is lost; the drop has disappeared, but the ocean remains as it was."

He continued, "You may break a mosque, you may break a temple, you may tear down any other holy place, but you must not break the human heart, because there the Lord himself dwells. Inside a temple an idol is worshipped, inside a mosque you worship nothing, but in the temple of the heart the divine light shines all the time. That is the true house of God."

The meaning of these statements were not understood by the *mullahs* (priests) and it was decided that he should be stoned. The saint was therefore dragged to the public square, and everyone who so wished, threw stones at him. Mansur suffered all of this in silence.

Then his friend Shibli, who was also a saint, in order to show compassion, and at the same time to test Mansur, threw a flower.

When it struck, Mansur winced and cried aloud in pain.

"Mansur, my friend!" cried Shibli, "Why did you suffer such pain, when it was only a flower that I threw?"

"Those who are throwing stones are completely ignorant of the truth, and know not what they are doing," Mansur replied. "But you, dear Shibli, know better; and that was why your flower caused me pain."

Three Men And A Circle

Once upon a time, a Priest, a Yogi and Mullah Nasrudin were having a conversation about God. They discussed many theological topics, and at one point they started to ask each other, "What do you offer to God each month?"

The Yogi drew a circle on the ground and said, "Everything I get, I throw in the air, and everything which falls inside the circle belongs to God, and everything which falls outside the circle is for me."

The priest also drew a circle and said, "Whatever I get I throw in the air, and whatever falls on the outside of the circle belongs to God, and everything inside the circle is for me."

Sheik Nasrudin said, "I don't draw any circles. All I do is take everything I get and throw it into the air and say, "Oh God, take what you like!," and then, whatever falls to the ground belongs to me."

Sometimes we think ourselves very clever. We dream up all types of complicated actions to perform, instead of simply surrendering everything to God. We should not think of God as a business partner, but should have pure devotion for him.

Ekalavya

Once there was a great martial arts teacher named Drona. He was very skillful in the science of weapons and became the teacher of the royal Kauravas and Pandava princes.

Hearing reports of his skills, kings and princes, desirous of learning the science of arms, flocked to Drona by the thousands. Among those that came to him to learn archery was the son of a low class tribal leader named Ekalavya. Drona, seeing that he was a low class boy, and thinking that he might one day excel all his high-born pupils, decided not to accept him as a student.

But Ekalavya, after prostrating at Dronacharya's feet, went into the forest, and there he made a clay-image of Drona, and began to worship it with great respect, as if it were his real preceptor. Doing this, he began to practice archery with great intensity and regularity.

Due to his exceptional reverence for his Guru and devotion for his objective, he became very proficient. Months passed and he would become so engrossed in the worship of the image that soon martial secrets would reveal themselves spontaneously from within.

One day, the Kuru and Pandava princes, with Drona's permission, had gone to the forest on a hunting excursion. A servant followed the party with the usual implements and a dog. When they arrived in the woods, they wandered about, looking for game. Meanwhile, the dog wandering alone in the woods, came across Ekalavya practicing archery. When the dog saw the dark hue low caste boy, his body smeared with dirt, hair matted and dressed in black, the dog began to bark at him. Ekalavya, desiring to exhibit his agility of hand, sent seven arrows into the dog's mouth before it could shut it and yet not harm it. The dog, pierced with the arrows, ran back to the Pandavas. When the princes saw the arrows stuck in the dog's upper teeth without harm they were filled with amazement at such skill and precision.

They immediately started searching the woods for the unknown archer. Soon they came across Ekalavya, who was still absorbed in continuously discharging arrows.

On seeing the strange looking person, they asked, "Who are you?"

The archer answered, "I am Ekalavya, son of the king of *Nishadas* (a low caste tribe). I am working to master the art of arms."

The Pandavas asked, "Are you the one responsible for these arrows in the dogs mouth?"

Ekalavya answered that he was.

"Where did you learn such skill, who is your Guru?," asked the Pandavas.

"From my teacher Dronacharya," answered Ekalavya.

The Pandavas were surprised on hearing this. Returning to the capital they approached Drona. Thinking that he must have been teaching that boy in secret they related to him what had happened. Drona was intrigued and went to the forest to see the boy himself. He thought, "I have always kept this secret to myself. How could another person learn it?"

When he arrived in the forest, Ekalavya bowed to his Guru with great reverence.

Dronacharya asked, "Who taught you archery?"

Ekalavya answered, "You did!"

"When did I teach you?" asked Dronacharya.

Ekalavya said, "I came to your ashram for instructions but you turned me away. So I came to this forest and prepared a clay image of you. Every day I worshipped you and meditated on you as if you yourself were standing in front of me. Through my worship of your form, in time, certain skills started coming to me spontaneously. Eventually I learned everything from you."

Seeing the boys devotion, Dronacharya was filled with wonder, and he told the royal princes, "This boy has learned these secret skills through devotion, whereas you would not be able to learn it even if I tried to teach it to you."

This story is narrated in the great Indian epic the Mahabharata in order to illustrate the power of one pointed devotion.

Imitation Of Holiness

A thief who was being chased by the authorities came to a temple. Outside the temple a number of sadhus were sitting, and in order to avoid the police the thief decided to disguise himself as one of these monks.

He sat quietly under a tree as if meditating. People soon started to approach him prostrating to him and leaving alms, fruits, flowers and sweets. He just remained silent. But after sometime the thief's heart was changed by these pious acts of the pilgrims. He thought to himself, "I have only assumed the garb of a sadhu, and look at how kind and generous everyone is to me. Who can say what will happen if I become a real sadhu!"

These thoughts affected him so strongly that he began to mend his ways from that very day and exerted himself to become a true sadhu.

Sometimes, even the simple imitation of a good thing leads to unexpected results.

Keep Your Money!

Once, Sheik Nasrudin needed to borrow some money and he did not know who to turn to. His wife, Fatima, suggested he try his cousin, a very nice man who liked Nasrudin. Nasrudin thought it was a great idea and decided to go and visit his cousin. His cousin lived some distance from Nasrudin, so it took some time to reach there. Along the way the Mullah started to think, "Suppose he will not lend me the money," his mind became full of doubts and he started to get upset. By the time he arrived at his relatives home he was very angry and was certain his cousin would turn him down. When his cousin came out to see him and welcome him, Nasrudin said, "For all I care, you can keep your money!" and turned around and headed home.

One should always remain calm, and never jump to conclusions. For quite often, difficulties and obstacles are only in our own minds.

Who Is Greater?

Once, King Akbar asked his Prime Minister, "Birbal, who is greater, God or I?"

Birbal, who was a wise man and understood the kings ego and told him, "You are indeed greater, your majesty."

"How is that Birbal?" asked the king in surprise.

Birbal said, "Your majesty, if someone commits a crime, you can banish him from your kingdom, whereas God can do nothing. How can God, who pervades everything, banish someone from his kingdom?"

The Fruit Of Immortality

In some parts of ancient India, when a devoted wife lost her husband, it was a custom that she would accompany him onto the funeral pyre.

King Bhartrihari was once telling his wife how he admired such a woman who had died in this way. The kings wife said that it was curious that this woman was able to live long enough for the pyre to be built and burned; she should have died the moment she had heard her husband was dead.

King Bhartrihari thought his wife's idea was certainly noble, but he wanted to test her devotion.

One day he went hunting and having killed a deer, he soaked his shirt in its blood and sent it to the palace, with the message that he had been killed by a tiger. When his wife heard the news, she fainted and died instantly. When the king returned to the palace and heard the tragic news, he felt extremely remorseful and sunk into a deep depression. However, within a short time he again married. But unfortunately, his second wife turned out to be the opposite of his first wife.

Some time later, a saint visited the palace and gave the king a fruit saying, "The one who eats this fruit, Oh king, will become young again."

The king, believing that his new wife was devoted to him, gave her the fruit as a special gift of his love for her. He also explained to her its magical properties.

But the queen was not at all devoted to him and was in fact having an affair with the captain of the guards. So, she gave him the fruit.

However, the captain of the guards was actually infatuated with a prostitute, and he in turn gave her the fruit of immortality.

When the prostitute heard of its qualities, she thought to herself that her whole life had been spent in sin, and if she ate the fruit she would simply prolong her sinful life. She therefore decided to give the fruit to the king, who was so virtuous and noble, and in whose kingdom everyone was happy.

When she went to the court and gave the king the fruit, he immediately recognized it.

"Where did you get this fruit?," asked the king.

"It was given to me by the captain of the guards", answered the prostitute.

The king sent for the captain of the guards and, pointing to the fruit, demanded, "Where did you get this fruit?"

The captain of the guards was reluctant to answer, but eventually told the king, "The fruit was given to me by the queen."

Hearing this, the king became reflective. He thought, "How contemptuously the queen repaid my honest love. She had a king for a husband and yet she went to one of my servants, the captain of the guards! He was also unfortunate. He had a queen for a lover, and yet he ran after a common prostitute. What kind of world is this, where such things happen?"

Thinking in this way, King Bhartrihari experienced great remorse, and dispassion (vairagya) arose within him. He then and there gave up his attachment to his wife and kingdom, realizing its futility, and devoted the rest of his life in the worship of God. He eventually became a great poet and saint.

Maya

Once Narada sought the Lord of the universe and asked, "Lord, show me that Maya of Yours which can make the impossible possible." The Lord nodded his consent.

Afterwards the Lord decided to travel and asked Narada to accompany him. After going some distance, He felt very tired and thirsty. He sat down and asked Narada, "Narada, I feel very thirsty, please get me some water from somewhere." Narada at once ran in search of water.

Finding no water near-by, Narada went far from the place until he saw a river at a distance. When he approached the river, he saw a beautiful young lady sitting on its banks. He became completely captivated by her beauty. As he got closer to her, she addressed him in sweet words and before long they both fell in love with each other. Narada married her and settled down as a householder, and in time they had a number of children.

They lived happily for a number of years until one year there was a famine in the country. Death was taking its toll everywhere. Narada suggested they abandon their home and travel somewhere else. His wife agreed, and they and their children set out. After traveling for some days they reached a river, but no sooner did they start crossing the bridge there was a terrible flood. The children were swept away one after another, and at last the wife too was drowned. Overwhelmed with grief, Narada sat down on the rivers bank and began to weep. Just then, the Lord appeared before him saying, "Oh Narada, where is my water? And why are you weeping?" The sight of the Lord startled the sage, and immediately he understood everything. He exclaimed, "Lord, my obeisance to you, and my obeisance to your wonderful Maya!"

Nasrudin Is Dead

One day Nasrudin happened to be in a philosophical state of mind and he was muttering to himself, "Life and death - who can say what they are?" His wife, who was busy in the kitchen, overheard him and said, "You men are all alike - quite unpractical. Anyone can tell that when a man's extremities are rigid and cold he is dead."

Nasrudin was very impressed by his wife's practical wisdom. Once when he was out in the winter snow, he felt his hands and feet go numb. "I must be dead," he thought. Then came another thought, "What am I doing walking around if I am dead? I should be lying down like a corpse." Which is what he proceeded on doing.

After about an hour, a group of travelers finding him lying there by the roadside, began to argue whether he was alive or dead. Nasrudin wanted to cry out, "You fools, can't you see that my extremities are cold and rigid?" But he knew that corpses do not speak, and so he remained silent.

The travelers finally concluded that he was dead, and lifted him up onto their shoulders with the idea of taking him to the cemetery for burial. They had not gone very far when they reached a forking in the road. A dispute arose among them as to which road led to the cemetery. Nasrudin put up with it for as long as he could, but then he sat up and said, "Excuse me, gentleman, but the road which leads to the cemetery is the one to your left. I know that corpses do not speak, but I have broken the rule this once and I assure you it will not happen again."

Sometimes rigidly held beliefs clash with reality. Unfortunately reality is generally the loser.

Jalandarnath & Goraknath

Once Jalandarnath, hearing of the greatness of the Siddha Goraknath accepted him as his Guru mentally. He than set out in search of him.

As he was walking, he saw Goraknath coming towards him. Of course he did not know it then that it was the famous Guru.

When they met, Jalandarnath bowed down to him. Goraknath asked, "Who are you and where are you going?"

"I am in search of my Guru Goraknath, so that I may do sadhana under his instructions."

"I am he," Goraknath said.

Jalandarnath asked, "Will you kindly instruct me?"

"Sit here," the Guru said. "I will return soon."

He than left, leaving his disciple sitting where they had met.

Goraknath did not return for twelve years. But Jalandarnath was already an evolved soul, and he continued sitting there, waiting with great devotion for his Guru. After twelve years Goraknath returned. But Jalandarnath had already attained full knowledge. Later, he also became a well known Siddha.

Ashtavakra and the King's Dream

Once, a long time ago, there lived a king named Janaka. Janaka was fond of knowledge and he supported many philosophers and holy men in his kingdom.

One afternoon, Janaka was comfortably sleeping on his royal couch. Servants were fanning him, and armed guards were keeping watch. He started dreaming that his rival, a neighboring king, invaded his kingdom and drove him into exile. In his wanderings he came across a corn field, and being hungry, he plucked an ear of corn and started eating it. But sitting nearby was the owner of the field, and when he saw a stranger helping himself to his corn, he ran after him and gave him two blows with his stick. The blows from the stick were so painful, that all of a sudden the king awoke from the dream. When he opened his eyes, he saw that the servants were fanning him and the sentries were keeping guard. But as he closed his eyes again, he found himself in the middle of the corn field once again.

Opening his eyes, he saw himself in the palace, closing them, he was again in the field being beating by the man. The king leapt out of bed and washed his face, but he became very reflective. There were some questions that he had and so he summoned all the holy men and philosophers of the kingdom to the assembly hall. When they were assembled, he posed this question, "Tell me which is real - what I have dreamt, or what I see now? When I was dreaming, none of these objects around me now existed. There were no servants or guards protecting me. But a farmer was beating me. I see now that I'm safe in this palace and the events of my dream no longer seem real. But which of these states is real?"

The holy men and philosophers were puzzled at the king's question, and wondered how to answer it. If they said that the dream was real, they would have to call the waking state unreal; but if they said that his waking experience was real, they would have to call his dream as unreal. Not receiving an answer, the king became angry. "I have been feeding you for so many years," he said, "but you can't even answer a simple question." He ordered that they should all be thrown into prison until further notice.

Now there was a young boy whose name was Ashtavakra. The name was giving to him because he was deformed in eight limbs. One day he asked his mother, "Where is my father?"

She told him, "He is in prison because he could not answer the kings question."

Ashtavakra said, "Then I will go and answer the kings question and free him."

His mother tried to dissuade him, saying he was to young, but Ashtavakra insisted on going.

When he arrived at the kings palace, he told the guards he wished to see the king. At first they tried to turn him away, but he said, "Tell the king that I have come to answer his question."

Soon, young Ashtavakra was taking into the assembly hall. The king and his courtiers were all sitting there waiting. When Ashtavakra walked into the hall in his deformed way, the courtiers all started laughing. They were amused that this misshapen boy should attempt to answer the king's question, which they thought so many others more qualified then he had failed to do.

Ashtavakra waited for the laughing to stop. When it subsided, he himself began laughing hilariously.

Now they were all surprised, including the king. Janaka asked, "These courtiers were laughing at your youth and deformed body, but tell me, why are you laughing?"

Ashtavakra answered, "Your majesty, I had heard that you and your courtiers were intelligent people, but now I see how stupid and foolish you all are. It appears you cannot see beyond the body. You laugh at my physical deformities, but you fail to see the Self which is the same in all. Those who cannot penetrate beyond the body remain stuck there. As for your question, I will tell you the answer: the waking state is no more real then dream, nor less real. When you dream, the waking state disappears, and when you are awake, there is no dream. Because one negates the other, neither are true."

He continued, "Who is the one who perceives the events of the waking state. Who watches all the events of the dream state and reports to you on waking up, 'this is what I dreamt' Who is the one who remains awake during deep sleep, when the physical body remains idle? That Being, the Self, which perceives the activities of waking, dreaming, and deep sleep, while remaining apart from them, is the real truth. Oh king, That is called Brahman, that is your own true Self. Know That."

Nasrudin's Lecture

O nce, Mullah Nasrudin advertised himself as a great lecturer and sold tickets. He was supposed to give a lecture on knowledge. People gathered at the lecture hall and awaited his arrival. When Nasrudin arrived he asked the audience, "Do you know what I am going to speak about?" The people answered that they did not know. Nasrudin answered by saying that there was no use speaking to those who did not even know what he was going to speak about, and he left.

The audience did not know what to do but persuaded him to give the lecture again. The next week they again gathered in the hall and waited Nasrudin's arrival. When the Mullah arrived he stood on the stage and again asked the question, "Do you know what I'm going to speak about?"

This time the audience answered yes. But Nasrudin then said, "In that case there is no need for a lecture," and left.

The audience became very confused and tried to think of a plan. They again persuaded Nasrudin to give the lecture. They gathered again in the lecture hall and waited for Nasrudin to arrive. Nasrudin finally arrived and again stood on the stage and asked the same question, "Do you know what I'm going to speak about?"

This time the audience had prepared themselves and half of them answered yes and the other half answered no.

Nasrudin said, "In that case, those who know should tell those who do not know."

There are many people who claim that they have achieved something and become teachers. But in fact, like Nasrudin, there is only the pretense of knowledge.

Is God Just?

One day two fakirs were sitting under a fruit tree. They had finished eating their lunch and then started smoking some *ganja*. The tree was very tall, and loaded with small round fruits. Next to the tree grew a pumpkin vine on a trellis. Its huge fruits hung down; yet the vine was ridiculously small. The fakirs each had a few puffs of ganja and began to feel its effects. As they looked around one of them said, "My dear friend, do you think God is just?"

"Of course, God could never be unjust," answered the friend, "Why do you ask?"

"You say he is not unjust, but look at that vine. It is tiny while its fruit is so big, then look at this tree, which is huge, yet its fruit is so small. Is this justice?"

All of a sudden, while he was uttering these words, a fruit from the tree dropped on his head and he screamed, "Oh God, there is certainly justice in Your world. If the fruit of this tree were as big as a pumpkin, it would have certainly finished me off without a doubt."

In The Name Of God

There once lived a great sufi named Shams Tabrez. He had reached the highest spiritual state of union and he identified himself completely with God. At times, when lost in that divine state he would shout, "I am God, I am That."

The people of his town could not understand these statements and would harass and threaten him with violence. They considered his statements as blasphemous, even though they considered him a saintly man in all other respects.

Once, a crowd of people came to his cottage carrying a young boy who had been killed by a wild animal. They said to Shams Tabrez, "You are a holy man, pray to God to bring the boy back to life, he will listen to you. Say, `Rise up in the name of God.'"

In this way they asked him to bring the boy back to life in the name of God. The holy man laughed, and said over the body of the boy, "In the name of God, come back to life!"

There was total silence but the boy did not revive. The saint said, "The child does not seem to respond to the name of God." He again called out, "Come back to life in the name of God!" But still the boy did not move.

He repeated the statement for a third time saying, "Arise, get up and walk in the name of God!" The child did not stir.

Then Shams Tabrez smiled and said with a soft voice, "Arise and come to life by my command!," the boy immediately arose.

The Greater Ones Come First

We are always told by great saints that the Guru is God, nay he is greater then God. To illustrate the truth of this teaching a story is related about a disciple named Sutikshan. Sutikshan was a disciple of the great sage Bharadwaja. He had great devotion for his Guru and did whatever his Guru asked him to do. He became well known due to his devotion, and soon Lord Rama himself came to the ashram to meet him.

When Lord Rama arrived, he met the great Guru Bharadwaja. They sat and spoke for some time and after awhile Rama asked to meet Sutikshan.

Sutikshan happened to be meditating in his small hut when his Guru and Lord Rama came to the door. The door was shut and the Guru called out to his disciple to come out. The moment Sutikshan heard his Guru's voice he got up and went outside. He saw both his Guru and Lord Rama standing before him. Both should be greeted with reverence. In India protocol is very important. One has to be very careful to greet people in the proper order, always keeping in mind the rule, 'the greater ones come first.'

The Lord Himself, Shri Ram, as well as his Guru, both stood before him. Who's feet should he touch first? Sutikshan was in a predicament. But in a flash he thought, "It is due to my Guru's grace that I have been able to have darshan of the Lord," and as he thought this, he bowed and touched his Guru's feet.

The Lord's Club

O nce, all the lords gathered together in a hall and decided to form a club, a club just for lords. Everyone agreed to the plan and hundreds of lords joined it. But at the first meeting the question arose as to who would be the cook, the butler, the watchman, the clerk, etc. This was a dilemma since they were all of the same class, all were lords. So who would do the work?

Finally, someone suggested that they draw lots. They decided to write down all the different positions to be filled on separate pieces of papers and put them in a bowl. One by one they all chose a piece of paper from the bowl. Whoever got the paper with cook written on it became the cook; the person who got the paper with guard written on it became the guard; the person who got the paper with president, became the president.

In this way the club was run by everyone, each doing the job assigned to them by drawing lots. This was repeated each week and the one who was the cook the previous week may now be the president, and the previous president may become the butler.

But even though they all performed these different jobs, they never stopped being lords. In the same way, we are all lords, children of the supreme Lord. It does not matter what jobs we are performing, that is just the lot we have drawn. The cook never thought himself to be a cook while cooking, he knew that he was a lord. The house cleaner never thought himself to be a house cleaner while cleaning, he knew that he was a lord. They were all lords, and these temporary roles they played were just an amusement for the sake of the club. In the same way, no matter what role we are temporarily playing, we should always remember that we belong to a great club, the Lord's club.

Don't Think Of A Monkey

Once, a man interested in mystic powers and the art of meditation approached a teacher. He asked the master to teach him the mystical formula by which repeating he would gain his desires. The Guru told him the sacred *mantra*, but he imposed a rather peculiar condition for its success.

"Don't think of a monkey!" commanded the Guru. "If you wish to be successful don't even let the thought of a monkey cross your mind while repeating the mantra."

Receiving these instructions, the man went home, sat in a quiet place and started repeating the mantra. But each time he did so, the thought of a monkey immediately came into his mind. He continued to try and concentrate on the mantra, but all he could think of was a monkey. In fact, the harder he tried to get rid of the monkey, the more he thought of a monkey.

Frustrated, the next day he returned to his Guru complaining, "Guruji, the thought of a monkey would never have occurred to me, had you not warned me against it. I have never thought of a monkey, not even in my dreams, but now I can think of nothing else."

Baba used to often tell this story when he gave meditation instructions. He would tell us not to set any preconditions for the practice of meditation. We should let whatever happens in the mental sky occur. By the very attempt to shut out certain thoughts, we become entangled in such thoughts. Instead, we should sit calmly and consider all that occurs within the pulsation of the mind as divine.

Sometimes the story would be told in order to show the need for the seeker to use his power of reasoning and discrimination while searching for a spiritual master. Instead of pointing to the divinity within everyone, some teachers have imposed the suggestion that one is a limited being. By the constant thinking that we are limited, weak, and ignorant; we experience ourselves as limited, weak, and ignorant. Once, the 19th Century Hindu monk Swami Rama Tirtha told this story while visiting the mountainous area of northern California. He was giving instructions on how children should be taught with love and sympathy. Whatever instructions we give the child, Swamiji said, should be accompanied by a clear explanation for the reason why it should be done. If one simply orders the child not to do something, they are giving an indirect suggestion to the child. To make his point clear to the Christian audience which had gathered around him, Swamiji recalled the Bible story where God ordered Adam not to eat of a particular fruit. "The very suggestion," said Swamiji, "created a desire in Adam's mind to eat the fruit."

Udhava and the Gopis

Udhava was a friend and disciple of Sri Krishna. Even though he was a man of wisdom (*jnani*), there was still a trace of arrogance in him, and the feeling of superiority. He thought that the path of knowledge was the only way to know the Self and he had no experience of love and devotion. Krishna had been aware of this flaw for sometime and had been thinking about how he could teach Udhava a lesson. Krishna knew that he could not confront Udhava directly about it, because his ego would have denied it. So Krishna thought of a plan. One day, Krishna said to his disciple, "Udhava, please go to Vrindavan and visit my childhood friends, the *gopis*. They have been missing me since I have not met them for such a long time. Knowing that I have sent you they will be very pleased to see you. They are simple folks and don't know much about meditation and the path of knowledge. Perhaps while you are there you can give some discourses on these subjects and thereby try to teach them something."

Udhava was very happy to hear Krishna's request and started out for Vrindavan immediately. On reaching the city he noticed a strange sight. The gopis were wandering around the city in a kind of dazed state. Some were crying while others laughed. Some embraced trees, and cows, calling out, "Krishna, Krishna."

Udhava thought them to be emotionally disturbed. He thought Krishna was right in sending him to them. He called out to them saying that he had come from Sri Krishna with a message. When the gopis heard Krishna's name they all ran to Udhava with great excitement. They asked Udhava all kinds of questions about Krishna's welfare. After answering all their questions Udhava started given them some instructions. He said, "You gopis should learn to meditate and develop your intellect by studying the scriptures. You must also learn to control your emotions. Sit quietly and repeat 'I am That'. In this way you'll come to know your inner Self."

The gopis tried to follow Udhava's instructions for some time and sat quietly. But soon they started dancing and singing Krishna's name. Tears of joy rolled down their cheeks and they embraced different objects taking them to be Krishna himself.

Udhava was shocked to see all this and he called out to them to control themselves. He said, "How do you expect to see the inner Self when you act in this undisciplined manner? Learn to meditate."

The gopis gathered around Udhava and said, "Oh Udhava, you have advanced far on this path while we don't know how to meditate, and know nothing about the scriptures. Through your sharp intellect you are able to separate the real from the unreal, but what can we do? We are simple folks who have given our all to Sri Krishna. We can think of nothing but him. When we remember him a surge of love pours out from the heart and tears of joy fill the eyes. In such a state we see only Krishna everywhere."

On hearing these words, Udhava's heart was moved. He thought, "These simple gopis with their pure love have won the heart of Sri Krishna. All along I have been thinking that I was superior because of my knowledge, but I now realize how much more advanced these gopis are." Udhava also realized that this whole drama had been set up by Sri Krishna to teach him a lesson. Udhava said, "Oh gopis, please forgive me. It is I who need instructions from you. You have advanced very far in the spiritual life, through your devotion you have achieved everything."

In this way, Sri Krishna taught his disciple Udhava an important lesson. That knowledge without devotion is useless.

Only If I Go

Once there was a great saint named Kanakadas who lived in South India. One day, during *satsang*, someone asked him, "Kanakadas, will I go near the Lord?"

Kanakadas said, "No, you will go only if I go."

Another person in the group rose up and asked, "Kanakadas, shall I go near the Lord?"

Kanakadas replied, "No, you will go only if I go."

In this way, a number of people asked the same question, "Kanakadas, shall I be able to go near the Lord?" But each time he gave the same answer, "No, you will go only if I go."

The people sitting there were puzzled at his answer and finally asked him, "Kanakadas, will you go near the Lord?"

Kanakadas said, "No, I will go only if I go."

This answer surprised all of them. They said, "Kanakadas, your answer to our question is very strange. When we asked if *we* would be able to go near the Lord, you answered 'no', and when we asked you whether *you* would go, you again say 'no'. What is the meaning of this answer?"

Kanakadas said, "When I say 'I', I mean the ego, the sense of I am so and so, which afflicts all of us. It is only when the ego goes that one is able to realize God. The moment this sense of 'I am so and so' vanishes, the Lord is revealed. Where there is ego, God is not. If you overcome your sense of separate identity, you yourself become the Lord."

The Wrestler And His Tattoo

A saint related the following story. Once there lived a wrestler in India and he was known by everyone as a great athlete. He had decided to get a tattoo of a lion engraved on his arm. He told the tattoo artist that he was born under the zodiac sign of Leo, the lion, and wanted two magnificent lions painted, one on each arm. Being born under the sign of Leo he was supposed to be a very courageous man.

When the wrestler finished given instructions on where he wanted them, the tattooist started to draw an outline of the lion with a small needle. He had started pricking just a little when the wrestler started breathing faster and started cringing at the pain. He said to the artist, "Wait, wait, what are you doing now?" The tattooist said, "I'm going to draw the tail of the lion."

Now the wrestler could not bear the pricking sensation on his arm, but not wanting to show his weakness he gave an unusual pretense saying, "Don't you know that fashionable people cut off the tails of their dogs and horses, so, a lion which has no tail is considered a very strong lion. So why are you drawing the tail of the lion? The tail is not needed."

"All right," said the tatooer, "I wont draw the tail. I will start with the other parts."

The tattooist picked up the needle and started again. The wrestler cringed and yelled out, "Hey, hey, what are you doing now?"

The artist answered, "I'm going to draw the ears of the lion."

The wrestler said, "Oh, you are foolish. Don't you know that people cut off the ears of their dogs? Dogs with long ears are not kept. Don't you know that the lion without ears is the best?"

The tattooist said all right, and proceeded to the next part. As he started pricking the skin, the wrestler again called out, "What are you doing now?"

The artist said, "I'm going to draw the lion's waist."

The wrestler said, "Haven't you read the accounts given by our Indian poets in their poetry? Lions are said to always be painted as having a very small and thin waist. You don't need to draw the waist of the lion."

Finally, the artist could not bear it any longer and threw the man out of his shop saying, "The lion is finished."

The saint says, "Here was a man, a great wrestler and athlete. He also asserted that he was born under the courageous sign of Leo and wanted to have lions drawn on his arms, but he cannot bear even the sting of a small needle. Many people claim they want God and want the whole truth in a moment. They want to accomplish everything and become Self-Realized in half a second. But when the time comes to get that lion (truth) painted in their hearts they cannot bear the stinging sensation and they hesitate, not recognizing that suffering is sometimes necessary for achieving one's goals."

True Renunciation

O nce a young prince went to a monk and prostrated himself before him. The monk asked him the reason for the homage he was paying him.

The prince said, "Sir, you are a holy man and a great renunciate. I know that before taking up this way of life you ruled over a large kingdom, and so I look upon you as a great being having renounced everything."

The monk replied, "If that is the reason for your honoring me, then I must wash your feet, I must bow before you Oh King, because you are a greater man of renunciation then I."

The prince was puzzled at the monks statement and asked, "What you say is very strange, how can I be a greater renunciate then you? You have given up the comforts of your palace, the delicious foods served there, your harem, and all your servants. How can I compare to you?"

The monk answered, "Brother, suppose a man possesses a magnificent palace and he were to throw out the dust and dirt of the house, would you consider him a man of renunciation?"

The prince replied, "No, not at all."

The monk continued, "Now suppose the man were to treasure the dust and dirt of the house but were to give away the whole magnificent palace itself, would you consider him a man of renunciation?"

The prince said, "Yes, if he gave away his whole palace he certainly is a renunciate."

The monk said, "In that case, you are indeed the true man of renunciation, because the Self, God, is the magnificent palace, your real home, and it is that which you have renounced for the dust and dirt of this world. I have renounced nothing."

The Sadhu and the Washerman

Once a sadhu was meditating on the banks of the river Ganga. As it so happened the spot where he was sitting was near the place where the washerman used to wash the village laundry.

Soon the washerman arrived with his donkeys and proceeded to unpack the dirty laundry. He started washing them and after some time he decided to rest for awhile. Being concerned about his donkeys, and seeing the sadhu sitting nearby, he called out to him saying, "Watch my donkeys while I take some rest," and he went and laid down under a tree and fell asleep.

After sometime the washerman awoke and noticed that his donkeys were gone. He went over to the sadhu and yelled, "What has happened to my donkeys?"

Hearing the yelling, the sadhu opened his eyes and asked, "What has happened brother?"

"What has happened?" yelled the washerman, "I asked you to watch my donkeys for awhile, and now they are gone, where did they go?"

The sadhu became indignant and said, "What makes you think that I was here just to watch your donkeys, can't you see that I am a sadhu?"

The washerman became infuriated at the sadhu's tone of voice and pushed him saying, "I had asked you to look after my donkeys since you were just sitting here doing nothing."

The sadhu pushed the washerman back and soon a scuffle broke out. The washerman was a stout man who got a lot of exercise from his work and soon he got the upper-hand on the thin monk, who ate little and irregular. The sadhu started calling out to God asking Him to help him. He kept calling but God did not respond.

Finally, the fight was over and while sitting quietly the sadhu prayed to God. This time the Lord appeared to him. Seeing the Lord the sadhu asked, "Oh Lord, I am happy to see you, but please tell me why you did not come to my rescue when that washerman had me pinned to the ground? I have been your devotee for so long, why did you forget me?"

The Lord answered, "My dear child, I did come when you called, but when I arrived I saw two men punching each other and rolling on the ground, and I could not tell who was the sadhu and who was the washerman. Due to anger and revenge the sadhu had become a washerman, and so I thought, 'Let these two washerman fight it out and decide the issue themselves.'"

A Miracle Worth A Quarter

Once there was a man who had acquired the power to walk on water. A real saint met him and asked how long it took him to acquire this power. The man replied proudly that it had taken him 17 years.

The saint, laughing, replied, "In 17 years you have acquired a power worth 25 cents. Since we give just a quarter to the boatman and he ferries us across the river."

Right Thought

Once there was a man who after traveling a long distance became very hungry, but he had nothing to eat. He sat underneath the shade of a tall tree and tried to appease his hunger by eating imaginary foods. He prepared a curry dish in his imagination and started eating it. Suddenly he opened his mouth wide, as if trying to cool a burnt tongue.

Now, someone passing by noticed this and asked what the matter was. The hungry man said that the food he was eating in his imagination had a very hot chili and it burnt his mouth.

The passerby said, "Oh brother, you poor fellow, if you had to live on imaginary food, then why not select something more sweeter then chilies? Since it was your own creation, your own imagination, why did you not make a better choice?"

In the same way this whole world is our own creation, based on our own vision. Then why not think ourselves to be great and fearless, instead of miserable and low? Why not think ourselves to be free and self-reliant, instead of bound and dependent?

The Prime Minister and Lakshmi

Once there was a prime minister of a king who went through all the practices required to invoke Lakshmi, the goddess of wealth and prosperity. He performed all the daily rituals and prayed with great intensity for her favor, but nothing happened. She never appeared to him, or blessed him, even after reciting her mantra millions of times for almost 12 years.

He had performed his practices earnestly but finally lost his faith and decided to renounce the world and its pleasures by taking *sannyasa*. The very moment he took sannyasa, the goddess Lakshmi appeared before him.

Seeing her, he became perplexed and asked, "What are you doing here? All those years that I wanted you to appear and bless me, you never did so; but now that I have renounced everything and do not desire you, you show yourself. What is the mystery behind this action of yours?"

The Goddess replied. "You yourself were the obstacle. As long as you were desiring me, you asserted duality and became a beggar. But the moment one rises above their desires, they are immediately fulfilled."

The Parrot Who Could Say 'Ram Ram'

Once there was a monk who owned a parrot. He taught the parrot to say; "Say 'Ram Ram' and you will cross all difficulties."

If someone visited the sadhu, the parrot would repeat, "Say 'Ram Ram' and you will cross all difficulties." People were surprised to hear even a parrot teaching others to repeat God's name.

Now the sadhu used to clean the parrot's cage every day, but one day after cleaning the cage, he forgot to hang it back up before going out. Shortly after, a cat came by and noticed the parrot's cage on the table. He started to harass the parrot by trying to catch it with its paws. The parrot became so frightened and forgot to say his mantra, 'Ram Ram.' All he could do was cry in terror.

Baba often use to tell this story at the end of a training course. He would remind everyone that we should not just memorize things like a parrot. But that we should embody the teachings into our very being.

When Shall I Realize The Lord?

Once Narada was on his way to Vaikuntha, the Lords heavenly region. Along the way he met two seekers sitting under a tree practicing sadhana. Coming to know that he was on his way to heaven to meet the Lord, they said, "Narada, you are going to meet the Lord. Please be so kind and ask him how long it will be before we reach Self-Realization."

Narada said, "Very well," and proceeded to Vaikuntha.

Narada reached the heavenly abode of the Lord and after having his darshan and asking the seekers questions, he left. On his way back home, he again passed the two seekers. The first seeker asked, "Narada, how long did the Lord say it would take before I reach my goal?"

Narada said, "The Lord said that you would attain Self-Realization within only three more life times."

On hearing this, the seeker became very upset and said, "Three life times? That is a long time," and becoming discouraged he decided to give up his practices.

When Narada approached the second seeker, the seeker welcomed him and asked, "Narada, how long did the Lord say it would take before I would reach Self-Realization?"

Narada said, "My friend, the Lord said that it would take as many lifetimes as there are leaves on this tree before you reach Self-Realization."

When the seeker heard this, he started dancing and crying with joy. Narada was surprised at this reaction and asked, "Why are you so happy, you have to go through so many more lifetimes before your goal is reached?"

The seeker replied, "Oh Narada, that may be so, but at least I now know that I will reach the goal one day, and that is why I am happy."

Our attitude should also be like the second seeker, who was a real seeker. Once we embark on the spiritual path we should have full faith in God, and be patient, no matter how long it takes to reach the goal.

Savitri

A story is told in the *Mahabharata* of the intelligent and virtuous Savitri. King Asvapathi of Ujain belonged to the solar race of monarchs. Even though the kings domain was vast, he and his wife were unhappy. For though they had been married for over twenty years they still had no children. They decided to perform the *Putreshti*, a special fire sacrifice to the gods in the hope of being blessed with a child. The fire ritual was performed and the gods answered their prayers. Soon the queen conceived and in due time she gave birth to a beautiful daughter whom they named Savitri.

As Savitri grew older she was educated according to her royal tradition. Soon the time arrived when her father thought of her marriage, but he was not able to find a suitable youth. Finally, he gave her the freedom to choose her own husband, and as a result she visited different cities and hermitages, accompanied only by her maid.

One day, while visiting a hermitage she met a handsome youth, the son of a hermit, and was struck with love for him. The boys name was Satyavan, and he too was filled with love for her. But neither Savitri or Satyavan expressed their feelings, choosing instead to keep their feelings to themselves.

Some months later, under the impression that his daughter had not found anyone, king Asvapathi called a council of the elders to decide if they should hold a *svayamvara*, or ceremony of self-choice, to which young princes from all the states in the land of *Bharata* would be invited. But as soon as the council had started,

Savitri approached her father and the elders and said, "Father, you need not think of a *svayamvara*, for I consider myself already married to a youth. You have heard of and seen Satyavan, the son of the hermit. It is he who is the chosen companion of my life, here and hereafter. It is he, father, who occupies my heart fully!"

Now the king and his councilors were in a dilemma at this news. How could a princess marry a son of a hermit? Brought up in every luxury of royalty, how will she be able to endure the life of an ascetic? Besides, would the hermit allow his son to marry beneath his caste?

While debating these questions there was a knock at the door. It was the sage Narada himself, the celebrated celestial hermit, son of Brahma, the grandsire of all the universe.

After receiving him with the proper reverence, and offering him a proper seat, they put their difficulty to him and asked for a solution.

Narada, to whom nothing was unknown, said: "Oh king, when you have heard my story you will agree that Savitri should not marry Satyavan. For this Satyavan is no son of a hermit. The old blind man, his father, who wears an ascetic's garb, is none other than king Dumatsena, himself reduced to this condition by his enemies. He was met in the field of battle and was conquered. Then, he and his wife were blinded and driven from his throne and palace. Here you see him now. But what concerns you most," continued the celestial sage, "is that there is a terrible curse upon Satyavan, and he is fated to die within a year of his marriage."

Savitri suddenly trembled at hearing Narada's statement, but quickly regained her self-composure. "Reverend father," she said, addressing Narada, "if it is to be as you say, let it be. As for me, I am at this moment a widow if you resolve I am not to marry him. I cannot marry another, for that would be a sin. One can elect a husband only once, not twice. In my heart I have given myself to him. Let me also tell you that I could bear widowhood for eternity after having Satyavan as my husband for a day."

Hearing this, and after some further deliberation, it was determined that Savitri should marry the love of her heart.

Soon Savitri and Satyavan were married and she moved to the forest hermitage of Dumatsena, where the couple lived together. She was an exemplary wife and an affectionate daughter-in-law, in spite of having discarded all of her previous luxury and comfort.

Month after month passed and they lived very happily. Satyavan was not aware of the curse, and Savitri did not wish to make her husband unhappy with the prospect of death. She had worshipped the gods daily, praying to them to avert the terrible decree.

Finally, the day before the predicted event was to occur, before retiring that night, she begged Satyavan to take her with him on the following morning on his daily excursion into the woods for finding fruits, roots, and fuel for the sacred fire. Satyavan wondered at her unusual request but consented to take her.

The following morning, the young couple went into the forest together. Savitri followed her husband like a shadow. When he climbed up a tree to pick fruits, she stood beneath with her eyes fixed on him, for there was no way to know at what particular moment the curse might strike her dear husband.

But no sooner had Satyavan climbed the tree, when he felt a terrible pain in his head. He was able to climb down from the tree but no sooner collapsed at his wife's feet.

"Savitri, my dear wife," Satyavan gasped, "I am dying. Oh what a pain there is in my head! Let it rest on your knees my dear Savitri!"

The next moment it was all over, Satyavan became unconscious.

Savitri did not cry, but remained sitting, holding her husband in her arms, watching for what might happen next. No sooner had Satyavan breathed his last than the messengers of Yama, the lord of the dead, came to take their victim.

But due to Savitri's great devotion and austerities, she sat holding her husband like a burning flame. The messengers were afraid to approach her and returned to their master voicing their fear. Yama was astonished at their inability to perform their duty and decided to go and retrieve Satyavan himself. Armed with his club and robed in scarlet, he mounted his favorite black buffalo, heading towards where Savitri held her unconscious husband. As Yama approached, he too felt that Savitri was no ordinary woman, and was struck with awe. But, he did not shrink from his duty, and gently approached Savitri.

"Dear daughter," he said in a gentle voice, "I am here to take your husband away: he is now mine. You must know who I am?"

"I know you by your words," she replied gently but firmly, "you are Yama. My husband may now be your property, and so will I be too: you may take him, but not without me."

"How can that be?" cried Yama. "Such is not my mission. You must part with your husband. The living cannot accompany the dead."

"You cannot convince me of that," answered Savitri, clutching the corpse even tighter.

Yama was extremely pleased by her devotion, and wishing to please her said, "Savitri, you may keep your husband's body, and I also wish to give you anything you may wish for, except of course, the life of your husband."

"If you are pleased with me, great Lord of the Dead, than grant that my father, who has no son, have one who will live to hand down his name to posterity."

"It shall be so," said lord Yama, "but go home now, for it is not good for you to remain in this forest alone."

Saying this, Yama turned and left, taking the soul of Satyavan. After going a short distance, he looked back, thinking of the poor widowed wife, and lo! there she was, following him like a shadow. "Where are you going?" cried Yama in surprise. "What good is there in following me, child? Go home!"

"Go home?" replied Savitri quietly. "Wherever my lord goes I go. I have no home but where his is. Oh King of the Dead, you know a true wife follows her husband through life and death. Even though you are a god, you cannot stop me."

Yama was struck by her great determination and devotion, his heart melting with pity said, "If I could, I would give you your husband back, but that is not possible. However, ask for any boon, and I shall grant it."

Savitri was very intelligent and thought for a moment and finally framed her request this way, "Oh Lord of the Dead, if you are indeed pleased with me, then grant me this boon; that my in-laws will be able to see their grandchildren eating sweets on gold plates."

"So be it," answered Yama Raj. Being extremely eager to please her, he did not fully realize the consequences of his granting her boon. Then, Savitri stood right in front of Yama's path, and smiling said, "Now please release my husband!"

"What?" cried Yama, "you are unreasonable, child! How can I return your husband?"

"Unreasonable?" answered Savitri happily. "Please consider carefully the boon you have just granted me and tell me if it can be accomplished without your returning my husband Satyavan."

As Savitri had no children, Yama perceived the truth of what she said, and he had to release her husband. He also had to restore the sight of her in-laws, as well as return their kingdom in order for them to see their grandchildren eating off golden utensils.

Savitri returned home with her beloved Satyavan. Her father-in-law was now no longer a hermit. The old king regained his sight and kingdom. But having lived in the peaceful atmosphere of an ashram for so many years, the king decided to retire and placed his son Satyavan on the throne with Savitri, a queen who was to be forever remembered for her devotion and undying love.

Baba used to often relate the last portion of this story whenever someone asked questions that were not thought out properly, or which tended to ramble. He would point out the benefits of first carefully reflecting on our questions, and then framing them in such a way that a great deal could be said with just a few words.

Nasrudin The Smuggler

Once, Sheik Nasrudin was engaged in smuggling. He would pack a donkey and cross the border into the neighboring country. The customs officer knew that Nasrudin was a smuggler but he could never detect the smuggled goods, no matter how well he searched the donkey. This went on for many years until Nasrudin finally retired.

Now, it so happened that the custom officer also retired and he happened to meet Nasrudin in a coffee shop. They greeted each other and started to reminisce about the past. Finally the custom officer said, "Nasrudin, it is now many years since you have retired from smuggling. I also retired a long time ago and can now do nothing to you. Will you not tell me at least now what it was that you were smuggling all those years?"

Nasrudin, smiling, replied, "Donkeys, I was smuggling donkeys."

Sometimes, even though the obvious may be right underneath our noises, we still don't see it.

The World Is As You See It!

Once, Lord Krishna was asked by the Pandavas and Kurus how it was that Yudhisthira was recognized as an embodiment of virtue, while his cousin Duryodhana was considered an evil man?

The lord decided to demonstrate to them the reason for this reputation amongst the cousins. Having gathered everyone in the assembly hall, Krishna called Duryodhana and said, "Oh Duryodhana! You are a great king and also a very intelligent man, please point out to me a virtuous man in this assembly."

Duryodhana looked around the assembly hall at all the kings and princes who had gathered there. He said to Krishna, "I can not find one virtuous man in this whole assembly. I see that they are all evil and arrogant."

Then Krishna said to Yudhishthira, "Please point out to me a wicked man in this assembly."

Yudhishthira looked around the hall and said, "Oh Lord, I can not find even a single wicked person in this assembly. All of them are virtuous and worthy of respect and honor."

Everyone became puzzled at the opposite and conflicting conclusion reached by Duryodhana and Yudhishthira. Krishna then explained the reason for this by saying, "The world is as you see it, one's own heart is reflected in the world. Therefore, the world appears to be full of virtuous men to Yudhishthira, and abounding in evil to the eyes of Duryodhana. According to the conditions of one's own heart, so is the vision of the world."

The Celibate
Who Got Married In A Dream

There was once a large ashram in the forest far away from the city. The ashram was full of *brahmacharis* (celibates) and renunciates who were very proud of their renunciation. It was summer and the rains would soon arrive. The head of the ashram sent one of his brahmacharis to the town to get supplies needed for the rainy season.

The boy went to the city and made the various purchases. After finishing his work, he decided to wander around the town and look at the sites. He had never been away from the ashram and was completely ignorant of city life. As he moved through the streets, he noticed a procession coming his way. Musical instruments were being played and everyone appeared very happy and jubilant. As the procession got closer, he noticed a boy and a beautiful girl riding in a carriage, both dressed in beautiful clothes and jewels. Not knowing what all this was about, he inquired from someone standing nearby. The person he asked noticed that he was a young celibate and said sarcastically, "You have been locked up in a forest ashram so long that you don't even know that this is a wedding procession. What do you know about this wonderful event. You have been wasting your time in the forest. These two worship Lakshminarayan, the lord of wealth. They are now going to become one and will enjoy many sense pleasures together."

The brahmachari was young and impressionable, and so the person he was speaking to completely filled his mind with thoughts of riches and the desire for sensual pleasures.

After this event, the young man returned to the ashram with the goods he had purchased. But after handing these over to his Guru he said, "Guruji, I wish to leave the ashram and am thinking of marrying. Please give me your blessings to go."

The Guru said, "Very well, you may go. I hope you will be very happy."

The celibate left the ashram and after walking for sometime stopped near a village well for some water and rest. He laid down near the well and started thinking about all the things he would do later - like getting married, having a house and worshipping Lakshmi the goddess of wealth. As his mind filled with fantasies of this nature, the young man fell asleep. As a result of such thoughts, he had a vivid dream, and in that dream he got married. His wife was very beautiful, and he was trying to make love to her. But, she was not in the mood and pushed him away. He tried to persuade her, but again she pushed him away. This time she pushed him so hard that he fell into the well. As he fell, he awoke from his dream. The well was very deep and he could not get out. He tried calling for help but no one heard his cries. So, he had to spend the night, not with a beautiful woman, but instead with water creatures. He spent the whole night groaning from a severe back pain, while remembering his Guru and the peace of the ashram. He thought to himself, "I got married only in a dream, and this is what happened from an unreal wedding. I wonder what would happen if I were to actually get married?"

The poor fellow cried the whole night. The next morning some woman came to fetch water, and hearing his cries they shouted for help. Many villagers came and pulled him out. Then they asked him, "What happened? How did you fall into the well?"

The brahmachari told them the truth, "I got married in a dream. I was trying to please my wife while making love to her. But she was not in the mood and pushed me aside. The next thing I knew I was in the well. I now have no wife, but only a broken back for my troubles." Being completely disgusted with the turn of events, the young brahmachari asked the villagers to take him back to his ashram.

164

The Barber
Who Wanted To Become A Brahmin

Once, there was a king named Vikramaditya. One day he called his barber to give him a shave. While the barber was shaving him, the king dozed off. Not wanting to disturb the king, the barber shaved him very gently. When the king awoke, the barber was already finished. He was very happy with the shave and told the barber, "You have done an excellent job. Ask for any wish and I will grant it to you."

In those days the learned *brahmins* were highly respected in the king's court and he used to be very generous to them. The barber was a simple man and thought that the highest attainment in life was to be a brahmin. So, instead of wishing for wealth or kingdom, he said to the king, "Your Majesty, please make me a brahmin. That is my only wish, kindly fulfill it."

The king said, "So be it. That will not be very difficult. There are many brahmins in my court who will make you a brahmin at my command."

The next morning the king sent for a few brahmins of his court. He said to them, "Take this barber and make him a scholar in three or for days. When he returns," commanded the king, "he should be a brahmin."

The learned brahmins were perplexed by the kings command, since they knew that they could not transform a fool into a scholar in just a few days. Of course, they could not tell the king this, and so they decided to hold a *yajna*, a fire ritual, on the banks of the Ganges. They prepared an alter and started the chanting of sacred mantras. The barber was placed in the central seat since he was going to be transformed into a brahmin.

As this was going on, the great poet Kalidas happened to pass by that place. Kalidas was a very intelligent man and highly respected in the kingdom. The brahmins told him of their difficulty and asked for his advice.

Kalidas said, "Don't worry, hold the finale of the yajna on the third day and invite the king to witness it."

The third day arrived and the culmination of the yajna was about to start when the king arrived. At the same time Kalidas also arrived with an old, and decrepit donkey. He tied the donkey to a nearby tree and started to rub its body with a rock. As he was rubbing very hard, the donkey began to bray in pain. But Kalidas continued to scrub and the poor donkey kept crying louder and louder.

Soon, all this commotion caught the attention of the king and those who were participating in the sacred ritual. As the donkey kept yelling louder, the brahmins found it difficult to continue with their recitation and stopped. The king asked, "What is the matter, why have you stopped?"

The brahmins said, "Your Majesty, we can not go on until that donkey stops its yelling. It is disturbing our chanting."

The king inquired what all the noise was about and was told that Kalidas was scrubbing an old donkey's body near the river. When the king heard Kalidas's name, he was intrigued. If it would have been anyone else, the king would have him punished immediately. But since it was Kalidas, the king knew that there must be some significance to this strange action. So, he went over to where Kalidas was.

As the king approached, Kalidas continued scrubbing and appeared to be completely absorbed in the work. Since the brahmins could not continue with all the noise, the king asked, "Kalidas, please stop for awhile and let the brahmins finish the chanting."

But Kalidas did not listen and continued scrubbing the donkey harder and harder, and the donkey kept braying louder and louder.

The king thought perhaps Kalidas had not heard him and stood right in front of him and said, "Kalidas, what are you doing?"

Not looking up, Kalidas said, "Please wait, I have no time to answer your question now."

But the king repeated his question. Kalidas looked up and saw that it was the king himself and said, "Your Majesty, I have to turn this donkey into a horse by this evening, and so I can not speak to you right now."

The king, with a look of surprise said, "Kalidas, what has gotten into you? Have you lost your mind? How can a donkey ever be turned into a horse, no matter what you may do to it?"

Kalidas said, "Your Majesty, what is it that you are doing? You are trying to turn a barber into a learned brahmin in three days, surely a donkey can be turned into a horse in a day."

The Guru's Test

Once, a seeker approached a Guru and asked for initiation. The saint advised him to retire into seclusion for one year and practice meditation and prayer. "After you have completed the year," the saint further advised, "and have completely subdued and destroyed your ego, come to me after taking a bath."

Having received the Guru's instructions, the seeker found a secluded spot and started his practices.

In the meanwhile, an old woman used to sweep the grounds around the saints hut. On the day before the aspirant was to complete his year of sadhana, the Guru called the sweeper and said, "There is a seeker engaged in meditation and worship of God living nearby. When he finishes his bath tomorrow morning and comes to my hut, you should scatter dust all over him with your broom."

The next morning, the seeker took his bath in the nearby river and proceeded to his Guru's hut. When he reached there, the sweeper, pretending to be sweeping the grounds, scattered dust on him as instructed by the saint. The seeker became enraged and started chasing after the sweeper trying to strike her and screaming, "You fool, didn't you see me coming? You are nothing but an ignorant old lady."

The seeker returned to the river to bathe for a second time. When he returned to the Guru's hut he said, "Guruji, a year has passed since you gave me instructions. Will you now bless me with a vision of the Lord?"

The saint replied, "My child, your ego is not yet subdued and anger still fills your mind. Go and meditate for another year."

The aspirant again retired into seclusion and for another year he practiced meditation and worship.

When the year was over, the saint instructed the old sweeper to simply touch the seeker with her broom when he finished his bath. The old woman did exactly as she was told. The moment the seeker finished his bath and approached the saints hut, she again pretended to be sweeping and as he walked by she touched him with her broom. This time the seeker did not chase her, but he became enraged and started to abuse her with harsh words.

He went to bathe for a second time and again approached the Guru. After requesting his blessings, the Guru said, "How do you expect to have a vision of God without controlling your mind? Even after two years of sadhana your ego still strikes others with poison venom. Go back and meditate for another year. But be careful, if you fail again, God will not bless you with His *darshan*."

This time the seeker returned to his hut and started practicing sadhana with great or determination. When the day arrived, the Guru instructed the sweeper to throw the entire basket of dust and rubbish on the seeker after he had taken his bath. The sweeper waited near the saints hut and when the seeker arrived, she threw the entire contents of her basket on him. This time, the seeker did not become angry, nor did he lose his composure. Instead, he joined his palms together and bowed low saluting her saying, "Oh mother, due to your kindness, I have freed myself from the grip of anger. I therefore thank you with all my heart."

After bathing for a second time, the seeker approached his Guru and humbly bowed. The Guru was pleased and blessed his disciple, who soon had a vision of the Lord.

Shuka and King Janaka

It is said that Shuka had learned the Vedas while still in the womb from listening to his father's daily recitation of them. From the start, the child was a natural renunciate. He used to spend time meditating alone and had full control of his senses. He had also learnt all the sciences from his famous father Veda Vyasa.

However, Shuka had not fully realized his inner Self. No doubt he was a great renunciate and had a very serious nature, still his father knew that he had some pride due to his great renunciation. His father therefore told Shuka that it was time he spent some time with a Guru, in order to know the inner Self. Vyasa said, "My child, in order to know one's true nature and for the purpose of achieving Self-Realization, you require a true Guru. Therefore, I am sending you to King Janaka for his guidance. He is a realized soul and will take you across the ocean of life."

On hearing this, Shuka was very disappointed, but out of respect for his father he did not show it. After failing to get his father to reconsider, he started for Janaka's capital. Along the way he kept thinking about this over and over again. Shuka was a great renunciate and did not own anything, except a loin cloth and a begging bowl. He could not understand why his father insisted that he go to see Janaka. Thoughts like, "Why is my father sending me to a king? What can a renunciate learn from one who enjoys sensual pleasures? What can a renunciate learn from someone who has many wives and is constantly engaged in satisfying the senses?" In this way he doubted any benefit coming from this meeting.

Finally, Shuka arrived at Janaka's palace and introduced himself as the son of Vyasa and said he wished to see the king. He was asked to wait while the minister went to the king.

Janaka told his minister to let the boy wait. Shuka sat down and waited, and waited, and waited. As time went by, he started to become quiet agitated. He started thinking, "How dare the king keep a brahmin waiting? What could he have possibly attained, one who is steeped in worldly pleasures? I'm sure there is nothing for me to learn here." Thoughts and doubts of this kind started to invade his mind. A number of hours passed in this way and still the king did not show himself.

Finally, Shuka was taking into the kings court. As he entered, he was amazed on how luxurious the court was decorated, with its rich brocades, silks and precious gems. There were actors and musicians performing plays, while beautiful dancers were dancing for the king. In the midst of all this sat King Janaka, lying on a comfortable couch being fanned by servants.

Seeing the young monk, the King welcomed him with respect and asked, "Sir, what brings you to my court?"

Shuka said, "Your Majesty, my father asked me to visit you so that I may learn something from you. Now that I am here I have a question for you, kindly answer it."

The King said, "Please ask your question and I will definitely answer it."

Shuka said, "You Majesty, this world is full of inequality and disharmony. On the one hand, a child is born, but somewhere else someone is dying. One person dances with joy, while another weeps in great sorrow. I have heard that you have attained equality-consciousness and are established in that state. What is the secret? Seeing all this, how can you remain unaffected. I see this comfortable palace and all these beautiful women surrounding you, as well as all these performers and actors entertaining you. How do you remain unaffected?"

The King said, "I will explain it to you tomorrow in a way that you can fully understand it. You will come to know through direct experience how this is accomplished. Now go and rest and return in the morning."

The King then ordered that the next day, all of the entertainers should perform their acts in the main street of the capital.

When Shuka arrived at the court the next day, the King ordered that a bowl of water be placed on Shuka's head and told him that he should walk around his capital without spilling any of the water. Then the King ordered four armed guards to serve as his escorts. The King said to the guards, "As he walks through the capital, even if a drop of water spills, cut off his head on the spot. Show him no pity."

When Shuka heard the orders, he regretted asking the King such a question. But Shuka was intelligent and remained silent. He accepted the situation and started walking through the main street. He walked very carefully, concentrating so that not a drop of water should spill.

Finally, Shuka returned to the palace and put the bowl of water down. He had not spilled even a drop and the King honored him. Then the King asked, "Holy Sir, did you watch all the festivities that were going on in the main street: the actors performing their plays, the lovely women dancing, as well as all the other activities?"

Shuka said, "No your majesty. I noticed no such activities. Knowing that my life depended on it, I focused my mind completely on the bowl of water."

The King replied, "Yes Shuka, you are correct. In order to save your life, you concentrated only on the water bowl, making sure none of the water spilled. In the same way, due to a fear of losing my head, I too move through this world concentrating my attention only on that inner state, and thereby avoiding being enmeshed by the pairs of opposites."

The Nectar Of Immortality

Once, after retrieving the Nectar of Immortality from the churning of the cosmic ocean, the gods decided to hide it so human beings could not find it. They thought very deeply about it since they wanted to hide it somewhere where it could not be found. Some suggested to Indra, the king of the gods, that they should hide it in the highest peaks of the Himalayas, but he said no, since one day many humans would climb it. Someone else said, "Let us hide it in the deepest part of the ocean since no human can retrieve it from there," but Indra said, "No, one day humans will be able to move under the oceans riding inside a vehicle." Another god suggested that they hide it on the moon saying, "No humans will ever be able to reach there." But Indra did not agree, seeing into the future he said, "No, humans will one day also travel to the Moon, and they will certainly find it there."

Not able to come to any conclusion, they approached Brahma, the creator. After saluting him, they presented their problem to him and asked for his advice. Brahma thought about it for awhile and finally said, "I have thought of a place where humans will never find it. You should place the nectar within the human heart, for no one will ever look for it there."

And so Brahma was right. Even though this nectar is so close to human beings, no one ever bothers to look for it within themselves.

The Power Of Destiny

O nce there was a great devotee of the Lord. He decided to go on a pilgrimage and started out for the famous temple in the city of Pandharpur. On the way he stopped near a village and decided to spend the night in a local temple. He started chanting God's name and it was done with such love and devotion that a couple who had then come to the temple were moved to tears. They decided to sit quietly and listen to him chanting.

When the sadhu had finished, the couple, who were now filled with devotion, invited him to their home for a meal. The sadhu thanked them for their hospitality but politely declined. The couple persisted and finally the sadhu agreed and accompanied them to their home.

When they reached the house the wife went into the kitchen and with great love prepared a delicious meal. The sadhu had his dinner and after was about to leave. The couple begged him to stay the night, and told him that he could start out on his pilgrimage in the morning feeling refreshed. The sadhu kept declining, saying that he would stay in the local temple, but they kept insisting. They told him that they would not get many opportunities to serve such a great devotee of God, and one could see that they had genuine respect and love for the sadhu.

Finally the sadhu agreed and they prepared a bedding on the verandah of the house and the sadhu laid down to sleep. The couple also retired to their bedroom, but soon the wife came out to the porch. She was very impressed by the purity of this devotee, and she became infatuated with him. She had a desire to massage his legs and that was why she went outside to the verandah. But the moment she touched the sadhus legs, her devotion changed into passion. The sadhu realizing what she was contemplating, tried to dissuade her, but she would not listen to reason. The sadhu finally told her, "Please, go back inside, I can't touch you. You are a married woman."

The woman was so overcome with passion that she could not think rationally. So she went inside and thinking that the sadhu would not gratify her desires so long as her husband was alive, she cut off her husbands head. She came back out and told the sadhu, "Now I no longer have a husband." Hearing this, and seeing blood on her hands, the sadhu was shocked. "You have committed such a horrible crime just for a few moments of pleasure?" asked the sadhu in disbelief. "No, I can not touch you.," he repeated.

The woman became furious and suddenly began screaming. The neighbors heard the commotion and came running and began asking what had happened. The woman said, "This scoundrel! We invited him to our house, thinking he was a great devotee, and fed him with great love, and then he tried to rape me. When I refused, he killed my husband."

The neighbors began to beat the sadhu. But there were some sensible men in the group and they said, "He appears to be a good sadhu. Who knows what made him act that way. Lets give him a suitable punishment and let him go." After discussing it for sometime they decided to cut off his hands and set him free.

The sadhu resumed his pilgrimage to Pandharpur, and he really was a true devotee and did not blame God for this tragic incident; he blamed only his own destiny for what had happened. Along the way he remained absorbed in chanting God's name. By the time he reached the holy temple all his karmas had been exhausted and he had a vision of the Lord. The Lord was very pleased with his devotee and told him to ask for a boon. The devotee said, "After seeing You Oh Lord, what can I possibly wish for? Having your vision is enough for me. However, if you wish to give me something, then please reveal to me why my hands were cut off. I don't wish them back, I just would like to know the reason."

The Lord said, "Your hands were the only obstacle preventing your union with Me. When they were cut off the final obstacle was removed." The Lord then touched the sadhu between the eyebrows in order for him to experience his past life. He saw that in his previous life he was also a sadhu. He saw himself bathing in the holy Ganga offering water to the Lord. Just then, a cow came running by. A few moments later a butcher came by and asked the sadhu if he had seen the cow. "You are bathing in the sacred Ganges," said the butcher, "so you must tell me the truth." The sadhu said nothing but instead pointed in the direction the cow had run to. The butcher chased the cow and slaughtered it.

After some time the sadhu died and was reborn as the devotee. The cow was reborn as the young wife, and the butcher was reborn as her husband. The sadhu who had directed the butcher lost his hands. The butcher who had slaughtered the sinless cow was slaughtered by his wife, who was the cow in her previous birth. The Lord said to the sadhu, "Now you have exhausted your bad karma, and so has the husband."

Baba used to often tell this story in order to convey the mystery of destiny, or karma. One can not foresee how one's karma is going to bear fruit. We may be happy one moment, but there is no guarantee that we will continue to experience happiness in the next moment. One's good karma may be operating for some time, but in the next moment our bad karma will prevail.

Peace Follows Renunciation

T he sage Vasistha, in order to teach his disciple the importance of a Guru and true renunciation, narrated the following story to Sri Rama.

Once, there lived a king named Sikhidhvaja. He was a charitable king and had many virtues. He appeared to gain pleasure from doing good to others. He also had a strong desire for Self-knowledge and had practiced some yoga. His wife's name was Chudala, and it is said that her beauty had no rival, and she also possessed many virtues.

The king and his wife lived happily without the least disagreement between them. They delighted each other in the passage of youth as if only one life pervaded their bodies. Soon mid-life set in and they turned away from their desires. Together they started to contemplate and reflect on life's meaning and the search for spiritual awakening. They started keeping the company of the wise and practicing meditation.

Chudala was actually more advanced spiritually then the king. She was always contemplating on the question "Who am I, where have I come from, and, where will I go?" She had a very sharp intellect and could pierce through the Vedantic meditation of inquiry, and was able to remove the sense of identification with the body. By constant practice the queen became established in the reality of her own inner Self. But even so, she performed all her duties very meticulously without the least longing for their rewards. Her mind was no longer filled with desires and she was untroubled by the pairs of opposites, desires or hatred. She was the embodiment of peace with a spiritual radiance about her. She had also attained the different yogic powers, allowing her to become a 'sky walker,' as well as enter the bodies of others.

The king noticed these qualities but did not have the insight into the queen's real achievements. He himself was unhappy not having had an experience of his true Self.

Even though the king had a powerful military, he was not happy. He had good subjects and a good wife, but still he was unhappy. He had advanced in the studies of the sciences, but this brought no peace. He was in pain because he had not attained God.

The king was overcome with grief. He undertook many religious observances, bathed in holy rivers and gave away various rare gifts, but he was still filled with grief. None of these actions brought him any peace. No matter what he did, it did not bring him peace. He asked many sages about how to attain peace, and the inner Self. The answer was always the same, "Peace follows renunciation."

He called Chudala near him and poured out his heart to her saying, "I've lost all desire for wealth and sovereignty and I wish to lead a forest life, renouncing everything. One who enjoys great wealth cannot enjoy that bliss which comes only to a mind free from desires."

To this Chudala replied, "Flowers begin to blossom in spring season, while autumn sees them yielding fruit. In this way our karmas begin to fructify in their due time." Chudala tried to convince the king that living in the forest would not necessarily bring peace. But the king had made up his mind.

The king left the palace in the dead of night and traveled until he reached the Mandara hills. There he built a hut made of leaves, prepared a rosary for the repetition of the mantra, a water vessel, and a deerskin for his meditation. Soon he had settled into a daily routine of meditation, *japa*, and austerities.

Many years passed but the king still found no peace. His queen Chudala, through her yogic power, knew where he was staying. But she had decided not to contact him right away. She knew that she could transmit the divine power into her husband and give him an experience of the Self, but she decided to approach him in another form, knowing that the king would not accept her as his Guru. She appeared to him in the form of a young brahmin named Kumbha-muni.

The king welcomed the young muni with great respect. Kumbha-muni inquired as to what the king was doing in the forest and what was he trying to accomplish.

The king replied, "I have renounced everything for the knowledge of the Self."

Kumbha-muni said, "You have a wrong conception of renunciation. Peace follows renunciation," after saying this he disappeared from the king's sight.

The king thought, "I have given up my kingdom, my palace, my wealth, and even my dear wife. Don't these actions constitute perfect renunciation? What more should I renounce?"

Then he thought that perhaps he should renounce the hut he had been living in, his wooden bowl, the deer skin which he had been using for his meditation mat, and the small piece of cloth he had been wearing. He built a fire and offered all these objects to it.

After performing this action, the sage Kumbha-muni again appeared. The king said, "Now I have renounced everything, what else is there to renounce Oh Muni?"

Kumbha-muni replied, "Alas! You haven't renounced anything yet. All your deluded renunciation are in vain. Peace follows renunciation," saying this Kumbha-muni again vanished.

The king continued to reflect and thought, "The only thing which remains for me to renounce is this body of mine. Made of bones and flesh I will offer it to the sacred fire."

As he was about to throw himself onto the flames, Kumbha-muni stopped him with these words, "What is this folly that you are about to commit? How, oh ignorant man, did this body of yours hinder your progress? How will death in any way help you? Though you destroy this body, still you will not achieve true re-nunciation. But if you will give up that which is the cause of agitation in this body, then true renunciation will result."

The king begged the muni to reveal to him the means by which the agitation of the body might be avoided. The muni said, "The wise say that the mind is the cause of attachment to delusive objects. It is the mind which is the germ of all actions and agitates the body like a tree when swayed by the wind. Therefore, Oh king, true renunciation lies in the restraint of the mind. It is only this renunciation which leads to the bliss of the Self. All other renunciation cause only suffering. The idea of 'I' is said to be the seed of the tree of mind. The sprout which at first germinates from this seed is *ahamkara,* the ego and sense of 'I am so and so'. This originates without form and is ascertainable only by inter-nal experiences. From this sprout the ramifying branches take their origin. Due to this differentiation, *manas* (mind), *chitta* (sub-conscious mind) and *buddhi* (intellect) are the different names, or qualities, of the one *ahamkara.* You should therefore jump off the branches of this tree of mind, and eventually destroy the tree at its root completely. The branches (impressions) will naturally produce innumerable crops of *karmas,* but if, with the sword of knowledge (*jnana*) you sever them from their trunk, they will then all be destroyed. Therefore, if through virtuous actions you destroy the idea of 'I' at the root of the tree of mind, then it will not again spring up. The renunciation of the *chitta* constitutes total renunciation. Nothing in this world really belongs to you, not even your body. Therefore, renounce that which you say is mine, since it is not yours, that idea must be renounced. You identify yourself with that and say that is mine. So you have a false identification. You should renounce only the idea of mine and thine. You don't have to renounce your body, or your life force."

After saying this, Kumbha-muni blessed the king by placing his hand on his head. Instantly the king went into a deep meditation, and realized his own inner Self.

We must understand the true meaning of renunciation. Through discrimination, reflect on what truly must be renounced. One should renounce the ego, which gives the appearance of diversity, and the feeling of mine and thine.

Nasrudin and the Elephant

O nce a fair came to Nasrudin's town and he decided to go and see the sights. Nasrudin looked around at the different activities and animals. When he came to the elephant's stall he walked around the elephant quietly, at times stopping, holding his chin and gently stroking his beard, as if in deep thought.

The owner of the elephants noticed him and observed him for sometime. He saw how careful Nasrudin was studying the elephant and he became suspicious and thought, "That man must be an expert on elephants, judging by the way he is observing that animal. Perhaps he is trying to find some defects with my elephants, and, who knows, perhaps my competitors may even have sent him."

The owner walked over to Nasrudin and said, "There is nothing wrong with this animal, here, take this 100 *Rupee* note, just go away and leave my animals alone."

Nasrudin took the money and went home. The next day Nasrudin went to the fair again. He went to the elephants stall and again started walking around it as he had done the previous day. The owner noticed him and thought, "There's that expert again, he must be greedy and has come back for more money." He walked over to Nasrudin and said, "Look, here is 200 Rupees, take it, but it's all your going to get. Now leave my elephants alone. There is nothing wrong with them."

Nasrudin again didn't say anything but took the money and went home. The next day Nasrudin started out for the fair once again.

When he got there he walked over to the elephants stall and again started walking around the elephant. He walked to the front, stopped, and held his chin, gently stroked his beard. He walked to the rear, stopped, and stroked his beard once again.

This went on for some time until finally the owner saw him. You could see that he was very upset. He walked over to Nasrudin shouting, "I told you I was not giving you any more money. Now there is nothing wrong with my elephants. You may be an expert, and may say that there is something wrong with them, but I'm not given you any more money."

Nasrudin said, "Brother, calm yourself, I'm not here to make judgments on your animal, or to spread rumors. I'm simply trying to figure out which is the mouth, and which is the rear. Since I have never seen such a creature, I can't figure out which is which."

Holy Water and the Copper Coin

Once there was a great saint named Vaman. His mother wanted to go on a pilgrimage and wanted Vaman to accompany her. But Vaman refused, saying that water can never purify the inner Spirit. His mother persisted, but he continued to refuse.

On the day that his mother left on pilgrimage, Vaman gave her a copper coin saying, "Dear mother, I know that you are determined to go on your pilgrimage, that is fine. I hope you have a good journey. But please take this copper coin and bathe it in the different sacred rivers and bring it back to me."

The mother went on a pilgrimage to all the sacred places. She bathed in the waters of the Ganga in Hardwar and Benares and also bathed the copper coin. Finally she returned home and handed the copper coin over to Vaman. As Vaman looked closely at it, he said, "Mother, this copper coin is the same as when I gave it to you. It has not become gold but remains copper."

His mother said, "My son, dipping a copper coin into sacred water will not turn it into gold."

"If that is true," asked Vaman, "then how can the body become divine by simply bathing in holy water?"

Baba would narrate this story in order to convey the futility of empty outer rituals. It is the inner attitude which is important. Baba certainly knew the benefits of visiting holy places, since he visited many himself, but what is most necessary is the attitude of devotion.

The Power of Chanting

O nce there was a government official who lived in the village of the great saint Ekanath. Ekanath used to have regular recitation of the Bhagavata and everyone attended the program except this man. One day, Ekanath saw the man and asked him why he did not attend the recitation.

The man answered, "I have so much work to do that I have no time."

Ekanath said, "If you don't have time to attend the readings of the Bhagavata, that's all right. But there are seven verses in the Bhagavata which contain the whole meaning of the Bhagavata in them. At least memorize those, and repeat them every day."

"When should I recite them?" asked the man, "I am always busy."

Ekanath said, "Recite them when you are taking your bath. I'm sure you don't have anything else to do then?"

The man agreed and said, "All right, I'll do as you say."

The man memorized those verses and every day, as he took his bath, he would recite the mantra. Days went by and the man continued his little ritual each time he had his bath. Finally, his time came and he died. His body was laid on the floor, ready for its last ritual. It is the custom in India to give the corpse a final bath before it is cremated. All of a sudden, the moment water was poured over his body, it became alert. It sat up and muttered the sacred mantra and then dropped down again.

Baba would relate this story to emphasize the power of chant-ing and the importance of daily recitation of God's name. The name has great power to transform an individual's life in a positive way.

The Blanket and the Bear

Once it was raining very heavily and the river was in flood. A bear had been swept away by the rapid flow of water and he began floundering desperately to save himself.

Two friends were sitting on the banks of the river and one said, "Look, there is a beautiful brown blanket floating down the river."

Without stopping to think, the other jumped into the river and tried to grab hold of the blanket, but the bear grabbed him instead. Both struggled to keep from drowning. The bear tried to save himself by getting on top of the man, and the man tried to push the bear down by trying to get on top of him.

Together they were being swept down the river. The man began to cry out to his friend for help, and the friend shouted back, "Let go of the blanket and come back to shore!"

"I'm letting go of the blanket," the drowning friend cried, "but the blanket won't let go of me."

Karma is like that bear, once it has grabbed you, it won't let go.

Nasrudin the Psychologist

Once, Sheik Nasrudin advertised himself as a psychologist. Someone went to him with the complaint that he could not fall asleep at night.

After questioning the patient for sometime Nasrudin said, "Before going to bed drink a glass of milk and eat an apple, and that will help you fall asleep."

After six months, the patient returned to Nasrudin complaining that his sleep had not improved. Nasrudin again questioned the man and then said, "Don't eat or drink anything before going to bed and that will help you fall asleep."

The patient started complaining and said, "What kind of advice is this? Six months ago you told me to drink a glass of milk and eat an apple before going to bed, and now you say don't eat or drink anything."

Nasrudin replied, "Fool, don't you realize how much progress psychology has made in six months?"

Baba used to love telling this story to show the folly of many modern ideas based on fantasies, and which appear to change with regularity. Often some people would point out to Baba how advanced modern psychology was, and questioned the usefulness of yoga and meditation in our modern culture. Can truth ever change?

Nasrudin in the Big City

Once Nasrudin visited a large city, and he was overwhelmed by the number of people in the streets. Fearing that if he slept and awoke again he would not be able to find himself among so many people, so he tied a balloon to his ankle for identification.

A practical joker, knowing what he had done, waited until Nasrudin was sound asleep, then removed the balloon and tied it around his own leg. He then laid down on the floor to sleep next to the Mullah.

The next morning Nasrudin awoke first, and saw the balloon. At first he thought that this other man must be him. Then he attacked the man shouting, "If you are me, then who, for heaven's sake, who and where am I?"

True Longing

Once, a man went to the sufi master Bahaudin Naqshband and said: "I have traveled from one teacher to another, and I have studied many paths, all of which have benefited me in many ways. I now wish to become one of your disciples so that I may drink from the well of knowledge and thereby advance in the mystical path."

Bahaudin did not answer the question directly but instead called for dinner to be served. When the rice and curry dishes were brought, he pressed plateful after plateful on the guest. He then gave him fruits and pastries, and again called for more rice, vegetables and salads.

At first the man was flattered, and as Bahaudin showed pleasure at every mouthful he swallowed, he ate as much as he could. When his eating slowed down, the master appeared annoyed, and in order to avoid his displeasure, the man ate practically another meal.

When he could not swallow even another grain of rice, and rolled in great discomfort on a cushion, Bahaudin addressed him in this manner: "When you came to me, you were as full of undigested teachings as you now are with rice, vegetables and fruits. Because you are unaccustomed to real spiritual longing, you interpreted your discomfort for more knowledge. But in fact indigestion was your real condition."

Many keep searching for more and more knowledge, but are in fact unable to digest any of it. The accumulation of information does not give mental peace, but mental dysentery.

Laila and Majanu

Majanu was the son of a washerman, and Laila was a princess, the daughter of the king of the land. One day Majanu's father asked him to take the royal laundry to the palace. While there, he happened to catch a glimpse of the princess Laila. On seeing her, Majanu became completely enamored with her. He was so overwhelmed with love for her that he was no longer capable of looking after his own daily needs. He could not think of food, how he was dressed, or what others thought of him. He had lost sight of everything else in the world. All he could think about was Laila. He wandered around the city with a dazed look calling out, "Laila, Laila."

When Laila heard of Majanu's love for her, she was deeply moved. She would see him from her room in the palace wandering the streets of the city crying, "Laila, Laila." Soon, she too became infatuated with Majanu. Even though their love had started with ordinary passion, gradually it became very pure.

No longer being capable of taking care of himself, others started feeding and dressing Majanu. The report of his condition soon reached the king and his heart was touched. He issued a royal command that all shopkeepers should provide Majanu with whatever he needed and send the bill to the royal treasure.

Now of course Majanu didn't want any worldly objects, for his heart was on fire with a pure love for Laila. But when the lazy vagabonds of the city heard the kings order, they all adopted the name of Majanu and began taking advantage of the situation. By the end of the month, the expenditures on Majanu had become very high. The treasurer complained to the king saying, "You majesty, this is getting out of hand, there may be a few Majanus, but it is not possible for there to be hundreds. Obviously others are taking advantage of your generosity."

The king said, "Leave everything to me. I will quickly rid the city of these impostors masquerading as Majanu."

The king then sent for the chief officer of the guards and said to him, "Send your soldiers to every part of the city, and have them make an announcement to all the people, that on the fifteenth day of the month, Majanu will be hanged."

When the soldiers made this announcement all the false Majanus panicked and finally disappeared. On the morning of the fifteenth day of the month, only one Majanu was left on the streets, crying, "Laila, Laila, Laila."

Da, Da, Da

O nce, the king of the gods, the leader of demons, and the leader of men went to Guru Prajapati, the creator, for instructions. They lived with him for some time as students.

Prajapati, in reply to their request to be taught, uttered only one syllable: "Da." He repeated the same syllable three times, once to each one of them and asked, "Have you understood?"

When Indra, the king of the gods, heard Prajapati's word "da," he interpreted it to mean, "control your senses," for he knew that the gods always yearned for sense gratifications. In fact, that is their only pursuit, for heaven is not a land of austerities but that of enjoyment.

When Virochana, the leader of the demons heard the word "da," he took it to mean, "have compassion," because he knew that demons were cruel and fierce creatures. Since this was the case, what they needed most, he felt, was compassion.

When the leader of men heard Prajapati pronounce "da," he recalled how greedy and covetous men are, how they are always spending their time accumulating wealth. So he thought the meaning of the word "da" was "give," give in charity.

Only one word was used by the Guru; yet three meanings were heard, inspiring three kinds of actions. To this day Prajapati gives the same instructions. The syllable is repeated three times 'Da', 'Da', 'Da'. Therefore, have self-control, give in charity, and have compassion towards all. This story was originally narrated in the Brihadaranyaka Upanishad.

The Architect and the King

There was a king who had a vast domain. He had an old architect at his court whom he trusted completely. One day the king called the architect and said, "Please construct a grand building. Since you are quite old, I would like you to complete it before you die. I'll give you a handsome reward."

The architect worked on the plans and the king earmarked a large sum of money to be spent on the building. He turned the entire amount over to the architect and asked him to work quickly.

Now the architect had always been an honest man but seeing the large amount of money, he succumbed to temptation. He started thinking, "I have worked so hard all these years but I am still not a wealthy man. I certainly deserve more then I have received." Thinking like this he began to plan how to use inferior material for the building. He talked the other workers into becoming his accomplices and they were going to divide the extra money among themselves. So inferior materials were used, but the king was charged for the best quality materials. But soon, they all began to quarrel among themselves over their share. Whatever money was left over was divided amongst the workers, but nothing was left for the architect. Out of fear the architect had to keep silent.

The building was finally completed and the king was informed. Many people were invited for the inaugural ceremony. Speaking on the occasion, the king said, "It is customary to give a handsome reward to the architect on the day of inauguration of such a magnificent building." Turning to the architect he said, "You have been serving me and my father for a long time. You have worked very hard. Therefore, instead of giving you a cash reward, I give you this building."

Dishonest tactics produce dishonest results. Whatever we think, speak, or do, we should know that we do it for ourselves. We alone reap the fruits of our actions.

The Dream

Once, three travelers on a long journey had become companions. They shared the same pleasures and sorrows and decided to pool all their resources together.

After a few days they realized that all they had between themselves was a piece of bread and a mouthful of water. They began quarreling as to who should have the food. They even thought of dividing the bread and water but were still unable to arrive at any conclusion.

As dusk was falling, one finally suggested that they should go to sleep. When they awoke, the one who had the most remarkable dream would decide what should be done.

The next morning the three men awoke as the sun came up. The first man said, "In my dream I was carried away to places so wonderful and serene that they can not be described. While there I met a wise man who said to me, 'You deserve the food, since your past and future life are worthy and suitable subjects for admiration.'"

"How strange," said the second man. "Because in my dream, I actually saw all my past and my future. In my future I saw a man of all-knowledge who said, 'You deserve the bread more then your friends, for you are more advanced then they. You must be well nourished, for you are destined to be a leader of men.'"

The third traveler said: "In my dream I saw nothing, heard nothing, said nothing. But I felt such a compelling presence which forced me to get up, find the bread and water, and consume them then and there. And this is exactly what I did."

The Loss Of Memory
And The Need For Time

Once Mullah Nasrudin had borrowed some money from his landlord. After about six months the landlord asked Nasrudin, "Nasrudin, you borrowed money from me almost six months ago, and have not shown any interest in paying it back. Have you forgotten about it?"

Nasrudin replied, "Sir, please give me a bit more time, and I will certainly forget it. But how can I forget it if you keep reminding me every month?"

Free Advice

Once, when the Mullah had become ill he went to see a doctor. He was staggering, and the smell of liquor was on his breath. The doctor said, "Nasrudin, you are beyond treatment, take my advice and stop your drinking, stop chasing woman, and go home early at night."

Nasrudin got up, got his walking stick and was ready to leave.

The doctor called out, "Wait, where is my fee?"

Nasrudin replied, "I would pay you if I were going to take your advice. As it is, there are people on every street corner who give such advice for free."

The Empty Handed Monarch

It is said that during the eleventh Century, King Mahmud of Ghazna invaded India seventeen times. Today Ghazna is just a small village in Afghanistan, but at that time it was one of the richest cities in Asia due to the enormous treasures that Mahmud took from Indian cities and temples.

When this cruel ruler was about to die, he asked his ministers to lay out all of his wealth so that he could look at it one more time. This was done and he was carried past it in a palanquin. After a number of hours of gazing at the piles of rubies, emeralds, diamonds, pearls, gold and silver coins and many other beautiful objects, tears began to flow down Mahmud's cheeks. Addressing his ministers, he said:

"How many tens of thousands have I slain, how many thousands of widows have I made, how many children are now orphans because of me. Yet nothing, not even the smallest piece of gold, is going with me now that death is near."

As the king realized more deeply the enormity of his crimes and the uselessness of all his treasures, he continued:

"When you take my body to be buried, keep both of my hands outside of the coffin, so that people can see that a great king has left this world absolutely empty-handed, and perhaps learn a lesson from my life."

The True Disciple

It is said that Saint Nizamuddin had twenty-two disciples, each of whom wished to be his successor. In order to determine which of them was the most sincere and devoted, Nizamuddin decided to put them to a test.

One morning he called them all together and said, "Come, let us go for a walk into the town and see the busy life of the city."

So they all walked to the town, and strolled around the streets and through the bazaar.

After sometime they reached the street of prostitutes, and Nizamuddin entered one of the houses. As he was going inside he asked his disciples to wait outside for him saying, "I have some work to do here. Have no fear. When the work is finished I will come out."

When he entered the house and the prostitute saw him, she bowed to the holy man and said: "Sir, it is my great good fortune that you have blessed my dwelling place. Please tell me how I may serve you?"

"I wish to spend the night in your house," said the saint. "If you can spare me a separate room I would appreciate it." He then added, as if an after thought: "Also, please tell your servant to bring me a covered plate with some cooked vegetables, some bread and a bottle containing syrup."

"I will do exactly as you wish," the woman assured him.

When the servant was bringing the covered plate, with the bottle of syrup prominently showing, the disciples saw it and said to each other: "Oh, this is a terrible sight! The Guru has lost all his merit. He now indulges in prostitutes, meat and wine." Convinced that their Master had deceived them all these years, twenty-one of the disciples left. Only Amir Khusro remained resolute in his faith to the Master.

The next morning Nizamuddin came out of the house and saw only Amir Khusro waiting.

"Where are all the others?" he asked.

"One left after you entered this house. Sometime later another left. And so, one by one, they all believed the worst and left for their homes."

"Why didn't you also leave?" asked the Master.

"Gurudev, I have no home except at your feet. Where could I go? There is no other place that I could call my home."

With great joy the master Nizamuddin embraced Amir Khusro, and told him that he would be his successor.

Glossary

A

Agra: A city in Northern India where the Taj Mahal is located.

Ahamkara: The ego; the idea of separateness; the sense of I-am-so and so.

Akbar: (1542-1605 AD); Great Mogul Emperor who ruled India from 1556 until his death in 1605 AD. He was a very liberal minded ruler, particularly in areas of religion. His court was open to men of all faiths.

Allah: The name of the One God in the Arabic language and Muslim religion.

Arjuna: The name of a hero in the Indian epic the Mahabharata, and the third of five Pandava brothers. The Bhagavad Gita was imparted to Arjuna by Sri Krishna.

Ashram: A place of refuge from worldly concerns; the abode of a saint or holy man; a spiritual community where spiritual disciplines are practiced.

Atman: The term used for the inner Spirit in the Upanishads; The real person.

B

Baba, or ***Babaji:*** Respected father; a term of affection for a saint or one's Guru.

Benares (also called Varanasi and Kashi): A city sacred to Lord

Shiva located in North India on the banks of the river Ganga.

Bhagavata: (Bhagavata Purana) One of the 18 major Puranas, or ancient books, containing tales of gods, demons, great kings and sages. They contain precepts of religious duty and worldly gain.

Bharata: The Sanskrit name for India, named after the famous ancient emperor Bharata; also the loyal brother of Sri Ram.

Brahma: The name given to the Absolute when viewed as the creator of the universe. He is conceived of as having his special abode in the realm, or heavenly region known as Satya Loka.

Bramacharya: Continence; a religious student who practices celibacy. In the wider sense it stands for abstinence not only from sexual indulgence, but freedom from all sensual cravings. Also, the first of four stages in life according to traditional Hindu society, the stage of studentship.

Brahman: In the Upanishads, God as Transcendental and Absolute is called Brahman.

Brahmana, or Brahmin: Literally, 'One who knows Brahman'; a priest, and one of the four main castes according to the ancient Vedic social system. It indicates the spiritual man of society.

Buddhi: The intellect.

C

Chitta: Mind, intellect, heart, the sub-conscious mind; As used in yoga philosophy, it indicates 'mind-substance'. It is comprised of the three subtle inner instruments of consciousness viz., the Intellect (Buddhi), the Ego (Ahamkara), which is the sense of I am so and so, and, the Mind (Manas), which is associated with the senses, and is made up by an assortment of thoughts and emotions. Actually, Chitta comprises all the levels of mind, and indicates the quality of awareness.

D

Dakshina: Gift; the gift or payment made by the student to the teacher for instructions; also, the sacrificial fee.

Darshan: Literally, 'vision, or seeing'; to be with, or have the sight of a deity, saint, or sacred place.

Dervish: Mendicant; a Muslim mystic; a sufi master; a member of a Muslim order of ascetics, some of which employ circle dancing and chanting in order to produce a collective ecstasy.

F

Fakir: Originally a term applied to wandering Muslim mendicants, but later the word was also applied to certain types of Hindu ascetics or yogis..

G

Ganga (also Ganges): The most sacred river in India today.

Ganja: Indian hemp; marijuana.

Gita: A song or poem, like the Bhagavad Gita, Guru Gita, Anu Gita.

Gopi(s): Cowherdess, cowgirl; The gopis were great female devotees of Sri Krishna, and were said to be incarnations of Rishis.

Guru, or Guruji: Literally, 'one who removes darkness'; a spiritual teacher or preceptor.

Gurudev: Literally, 'the divine Guru'; God as Guru; an affectionate, yet respectful term used to address one's Guru.

H

Hardwar: Literally, 'the doorway to God'; a famous town and pilgrimage center located at the foothills of the Himalayas.

Hari: 'The Remover of sins'; a name of God.

Hatha Yogi: One who practices Hatha Yoga, which is made up of various physical postures and breathing techniques.

I

Indra: The powerful, or mighty; the king, lord or chief of the gods; Vedic god of rain and thunder.

J

Japa: The devotional repetition of the *mantra*, often while counting on a rosary. For the purpose of meditation, japa is usually performed silently.

Jnana: Enlightened wisdom; the highest yogic knowledge; the knowledge of the Absolute Reality leading to freedom from phenomenal life.

K

Karma: Action or deed, both mental and physical; the law of cause and effect; the reservoir of past impressions; the belief that an individual will reap the fruits of their own past actions, whether in the present life or in some future one; results of one's past actions; destiny; in Vedic times the word was also used to indicate sacred fire rituals (*yajna*).

Koran: The sacred Scripture of Islam revealed to the prophet Mohammed.

Krishna: Literally, blue-black, or dark colored; The central figure in the Indian epic, the Mahabharata, of which the Bhagavad Gita forms one chapter. Krishna is considered an incarnation (*Avatara*) of God.

Kubera: The god of riches and treasures; the treasurer of the celestials.

Kauravas: From Kuru; an ancient clan, and the ancestors of both the Pandavas and Kauravas in the Mahabharata epic. However, the name has been applied mainly to the cousins, and enemies of the Pandavas, headed by Duryodhana.

L

Lakshmi: The beautiful; one having auspicious marks; the goddess of wealth and prosperity.

M

Maharaja: Literally, 'great king', or 'prince'; an Indian title for a great king (*raja*); one ranked above a normal raja; also, a term of address of great Gurus or holy men.

Mahabharata: Also known simply as *Bharata;* The great Indian epic attributed to sage Vyasa. It relates the story, and conflicts, between the Pandava and Kaurava cousins. It is composed in 100,000 verses, which is seven times the size of the Iliad and Odyssey combined.

Maharashtra: The Indian state where King Shivaji ruled.

Mahout: An elephant trainer and controller; the keeper and driver of an elephant.

Manas: The mind; that which is associated with the senses, and is made up by an assortment of thoughts and emotions.

Mantra: 'instrument of thought'; a mystical or sacred word, verse, or formula, given by the Guru at the time of initiation. When given by a true Guru it is considered to be a 'conscious' mantra, and becomes a vehicle for the transmission of the Guru's spiritual power.

Maya: The inscrutable, mysterious, and magical power of God (Brahman) which is responsible for the perception of diversity.

Mosque: A Muslim house of worship; a gathering place for religious worship and instructions.

Mullah: A Muslim religious teacher or leader; also used as a title.

Muni: A sage; one who is silent, or rarely speaks.

Musa: The Arabic name for Moses.

N

Narada: An ancient sage and devotee of Vishnu (God); The seer of a number of hymns of the Rigveda and author of several other works, including the Bhakti-Sutras, or aphorisms on Devotion.

O

Om: The 'Word'; in Hinduism, the mystical and sacred syllable representing the Absolute (Brahman).

Om Namah Shivaya: Salutations (or homage, adoration) to Shiva (God); I bow to Shiva; The great mantra of Shaivism known as the 'Panchakshari', or 'five syllable' mantra, which is found in the Krishna Yajur Veda.

P

Pandavas: From *Pandu;* The heroes of the great Indian epic the Mahabharata. The five Pandavas were Yudhishthira, Bhima, Arjuna, Nakula and Sahadeva.

Pandharpur: A town located in India in the state of Maharashtra, and which is considered a great place of pilgrimage.

Prajapati: Literally, 'Lord of Creatures'; God as creator.

Pundit: A scholar; a learned man; an authority or critic.

R

Raja: King

Rama: Hero of the great Indian epic poem, the Ramayana, composed in Sanskrit by the poet Valmiki. Sri Rama is believed to be the 7th incarnation (*Avatara*) of Vishnu (God).

Rupee: Indian currency.

S

Sadhu: The holy, or righteous; an ascetic, or holy man. From *sadh*, meaning 'one who goes straight to the goal.'

Sannyasi: (or sannyasin) Literally, one who 'throws down' or 'abandons'; one who has renounced or abandoned the worldly life in favor of the monastic life. Sannyasa is a personal dedication to the path of God-Realization and service to humanity.

Shanti: Peace, calm, mental tranquillity, mental peace.

Shiva: Literally, 'the auspicious, kind, and compassionate One'; The name given to the Absolute when viewed as the dissolver of the universe; The Supreme Lord who is transcendent as well as immanent; He is conceived as having his special abode in the realm, or heavenly region known as Kailasa.

Siddha: One who has perfected or accomplished the goal. A perfected spiritual master of great purity and power.

Sufi: An Arabic word for the mystics within the religion of Islam. From 'suf', meaning wool, indicating the simple woolen robe worn by the Sufis.

Swami, or Swamiji: Lord; 'One who is lord of his senses'; he who knows himself; a religious title of a Hindu holy man, usually a sannyasi; a term of respect.

Synagogue: A Jewish house of worship; a place of meeting for Jewish worship and religious instructions.

U

Upanishad: Literally, 'sitting near'; also meaning, 'esoteric knowledge'; The scriptures embodying the teachings of the ancient sages of India, and which are a part of the Vedas. There are 108 Upanishads.

V

Vaikuntha: Heaven; the celestial realm or abode of Vishnu (God).

Vedas: The primary scriptures of the Hindus, which are believed to be eternal.

Vedanta: Literally, 'the end of the Vedas'; Vedic philosophy or knowledge indicating ultimate wisdom; one of the six orthodox schools of Indian philosophy, arising from discussions in the Upanishads about the nature of the Absolute. The three main scriptures of this philosophy are: the Upanishads, Brahma Sutras, and the Bhagavad Gita.

Vishnu: A name given to the Absolute when viewed as the sustainer of the universe. He is conceived of as having his special abode in the realm, or heavenly region known as Vaikuntha.

Vyasa: Literally, 'the compiler'; A great sage who is credited with compiling the four Vedas, and is the author of the epic the Mahabharata, as well as all the Puranas. He was the son of sage Parashara, and had a son named Shukadev muni. His given name was Krishna Dwaipayana.

Y

Yama: the 'Restrainer'; The name of the god of death. He is also known as the god of justice (Dharma).

Yoga: From '*yuj*', to yoke or join; One of the six systems of Hindu philosophy. Yoga teaches the means by which the individual spirit can be joined or united with the Universal Spirit.

Yoga Sutras: 'Aphorisms on yoga'; A systematic treatise on yoga by the sage Patanjali.

Yogi: One (a male) who practices yoga; also, one who has achieved yoga, or spiritual union; a female practitioner is called a *Yogini*.